DATE DUE			
Jan 21 '74			
Apr 5 '76			
Dec 12 '80			
Apr 27 '83			

Military Power
and Potential

Military Power and Potential

Klaus Knorr   Princeton University

Heath Lexington Books
D. C. Heath and Company
Lexington, Massachusetts

Library of Congress Number: 71-108787

Contents

Economic Capacity

Administrative Capabilities

The Political Foundations of Military Power

Preface

During the early 1950's I wrote a book on *The War Potential of Nations* which was published in 1955 by the Princeton University Press. Some years ago I began to think that I should undertake another study of this subject, since I had become aware of some flaws in my first book. The fact that this book had been made by World War II contributed especially to its limitations. Over the past two decades, the components and conditions of military power, and the environment in which it is exerted, have undergone drastic change, and it now seemed desirable to review the subject from the perspective of the late 1960's. I was also tempted by the thought that recent progress in the social sciences would permit me to improve the analysis of several aspects of military potential. I began writing the new book in 1968. It is not a revision of the old book. In fact I rarely consulted the latter when writing the new one. Although some of the basic concepts are the same, what emerged is essentially a different book.

One point made repeatedly in the following study is that the military potential of states varies with different forms and purposes of military power. Thus, a state's potential for producing military strength for *domestic* use is apt to differ somewhat from its potential for developing military strength for international employment. The present study is concerned exclusively with potential for *international* military power.

I am grateful for the research facilities made available to me by the Center of International Studies at Princeton University.

Klaus Knorr

1 Military Power: Nature, Components and Functions

When sovereign nation-states pursue interests which clash with those of other states, and take action to achieve the most satisfactory (or least unsatisfactory) outcome of the resulting interstate conflict, they will usually attempt to exert influence on each other's behavior. Some of the means they will use for this purpose are coercive; that is, they are threats or actions aimed at depriving the other party of something it values, such as territory, independence, peace, trade, prestige, or self-respect. Means are non-coercive when one government offers another the continuation or an increment of something it values, such as diplomatic and military support, cessation of hostilities, financial aid, or export markets. Threats are made and benefits offered in order to produce certain intended effects on the behavior of the addressee. A wants B to do X, or to refrain from doing Y; therefore A threatens B with punishments or offers him rewards. However, governments may also influence other states without offering rewards or using coercion. They may be able to do so by giving information, for example, by explaining the purposes or implications of their own policies which contributed to the conflict, for these may have been misunderstood. Coercive and non-coercive means, and information, may be used simultaneously in various combinations.

Throughout recorded history, sovereign states have employed military power as one means of coercion, usually in combination with other means of influence. However, military power can be used for other than coercive purposes. It has been, and can be, used to take or defend something forcibly, for example a city or province, or to exterminate an enemy. In this case, no attempt is made to influence the opponent. The object is simply to take or withhold something from him by sheer force.[1] Sufficient military strength, and the will to use it, is all that is needed to achieve the objective. When military force is employed in war, it is often, if not usually, for both purposes; that is, to take or defend some objects forcibly, and—by threatening the opponent with further destruction—to influence him toward terminating hostilities on certain terms, or toward accepting surrender.

Even when military power is used as a means of influence, its employment is not always coercive. It can be used in order to offer utilities to another state, as when an alliance is proposed. Our focus, however, will be on the use of military power to threaten some other state with disutilities, or to inflict actual violence on it, since the employment of power as a benefit to one state rests on the possibility of its use as a means of coercion against another.

In applying this focus, the use of military strength is not regarded as standing in contrast to the employment of diplomatic negotiation or other government communications. The use of force is only part of the process of reconciling interstate interests when they are in sharp conflict, and even then the resort to force is a matter of choice. Where the choice to use force is made, the aim is usually agreement. The weight of military force is thrown into the scales when other communication is expected to lack sufficient impact.

Since the purpose of this chapter is to introduce the examination of military potential which is to follow, its scope is restricted accordingly. The following discussion will concentrate on the military power, putative and actualized, of single states vis-à-vis other single states. However, this analysis could be extended readily in several directions. As indicated by frequent references to foreign support and the possibility of third-party intervention, the analysis could be extended to cover military power relationships between groups of states. It could be extended further to consider the impact of different patterns in the international distribution of power, such as the classical balance-of-power system, or the bipolar pattern which emerged following World War II. Finally, it could be extended by examining the role of military power, putative or actualized, when it becomes effective in conjunction with other means of international influence, whether coercive or non-coercive. Such an extension would open the way to a study of crisis bargaining.

The Concept of Military Power

Like all means of influence, the concept of military power as a capacity for exercising coercion is not as clearcut as it looks on first

---

[1] For the most lucid exposition of this distinction, see Thomas C. Schelling, *Arms and Influence* (New Haven: Yale University Press, 1966), Ch. I.

notice.[2] If power is defined as the ability to affect behavior, the concept can then be interpreted in two alternative ways, each of which captures a different aspect of reality. One interpretation equates power with actual influence. Power then exists only as influence is achieved, and is measurable only in terms of visible changes in behavior patterns. We will call this *actualized power.* According to the second interpretation, power is the *ability* to coerce in order to exercise influence. In this meaning, power is only the potential cause of behavioral changes; it preexists the actual achievement of influence. We will call this *putative power.* Actualized power is generated in the influence process and exists only within a specific relationship between states. Putative power is something which pertains to particular states; it is something they possess, and which they may use or not use. Putative power is a means; actualized power is an effect. Henceforth, when we simply refer to military power, we mean putative power which, however, is a capacity for taking or defending objects forcibly as well as a means to exercise coercion.

The notion of power does not specify purely unilateral power by one state over another. Most power relationships are characterized by some degree of reciprocity. Hence, when we speak of A exerting power on B, we refer to net power.

Mechanisms of Effectiveness

There are three mechanisms through which the military power of one state may affect the behavior of other states. One mechanism is resort to war—that is, organized violence between collective groups, especially state-organized forces—to the extent that hostilities have the purpose of affecting the opponent's behavior (*i.e.,* to the extent that the object of force is not simply seizure or denial of a valuable object). The second mechanism is the *threat* of military action, including war, or of the expansion of ongoing hostilities. The third is through the *anticipation* by states that another state may proceed to use its military forces in the event of a serious dispute.

This third mechanism is very important in the relations of states since its operation is less discontinuous and more pervasive than actual warfare or the use of specific military threats. A government, in shaping its policy toward a state perceived to be not only militarily superior but also apt to use its military force, will take these conditions tacitly into consideration even though no specific military threat has been uttered. It will simply reject, or not even consider,

[2] *Cf.* Robert A. Dahl, "The Concept of Power," *Behavioral Science,* II (1957), pp. 201–215; John C. Harsanyi, "Measurement of Social Power, Opportunity Costs, and the Theory of Two-Person Bargaining Games," *Behavorial Science,* VII (1962), pp. 67–68; William H. Riker, "Some Ambiguities in the Notion of Power," *The American Political Science Review,* LVIII (1964), pp. 341–349; Jack H. Nagel, "Some Questions About the Concept of Power," *Behavioral Science,* XXIII (1968), pp. 129–137.

certain choices of action. If this happens, the military power of the stronger state has been effective in influencing the behavior of other states even without deliberate attempts to do so. The putative power of the superior state has then become actualized.

Conditions of Effectiveness

In inquiring further into the nature of military power, both putative and actualized, we begin, for reasons of expository convenience, by discussing the third mechanism of effectiveness first, and then the second and first. In the analysis which follows, we will look into the military power relationships between two states, A and B.

According to the third mechanism of anticipated force, State B may be influenced by its expectation that, if it does X rather than Y, State A may with some probability resort to its military power. But exactly what determines A's putative military power? This results from three factors: its actual military capabilities, its capacity for increasing these capabilities in a crisis, and its military reputation.

The effectiveness of a state's military forces or capabilities depends on their size, composition, equipment, logistical reach, and availability for new application. Military forces are not a homogeneous entity with which different states are endowed in varying amounts. As will be examined in more detail below, states may have forces more suitable for some modes and theaters of war than for others. For example, a state may possess a strong capability to deter a nuclear attack by another state but lack strong forces for waging conventional combat. Or its forces may be strong for defense of its territory but lack of the logistical capacity for large-scale operations in far away places. Thus, the very composition of a nation's armed forces conditions the scope of its military power. Even though a state has impressive armed forces, they may be partly, or wholly committed to certain uses and, to that extent, unavailable for different types of conflict. Regarding new uses of military strength, only those forces count which can be allocated for them. In general, the armed forces of great military powers have larger size, more versatility, wider geographic reach, and are capable of greater, and more varied expansion than those of lesser military powers. But sheer scarcity of resources places limitations even on the capabilities of great and wealthy military powers.

Related to the size, equipment and reach of a state's military forces is its military potential, that is, its ability to increase these forces in a crisis or in war. States differ in the magnitude and composition of resources convertible into additional military capabilities, in the speed and versatility with which conversion can take place, and in the degree to which governments are able to commit resources to this purpose.

But although military forces, both actual and potential, are vital conditions of military power, military forces and putative military power are not the same thing. Armies, air forces, and navies are instruments of military power—capabilities from which power may be derived. They are a necessary but not a sufficient condition of military power. Another essential condition is a state's recognized willingness to employ military force on behalf of interests it deems important enough to justify the costs of such employment. In short, this power rests also on A's military reputation—an intangible asset—which is based, in turn, on its previous military and crisis behavior, and on the absence of new evidence which would counsel a discounting of past behavior. The more readily a state has resorted to force in the past, in general or in specifically relevant situations, the more credible that it will do so in the future. However, events such as changes in government or political regime can lead to revisions in a state's military reputation.

If such is the nature of A's putative military power, it becomes actualized when B anticipates a possible military threat by A if it (B) undertakes a course of action sharply countering some sufficiently vital interests of A. The actualization of A's power also depends upon additional factors, indicated by the following questions with which B's government will be concerned:

1. What are the chances that A will proceed to a military threat in the course of the dispute which will ensue?
2. What sort of threat will it be?
3. How vulnerable militarily are we to it?
4. What kind of support can we expect, or manage to evoke, at home and abroad?
5. How does the value of our intended action compare with the risks of receiving a military threat?

This list indicates the conditionality of A's actualized power; and such conditionality explains why, even though states perceive and consider differences in their military power, militarily weak states have usually had considerable freedom of action in countering the interests of stronger states. Thus, although A may be a strong military power in its region, the geographic reach of its military forces may be small, and hence will not impress small powers located at a considerable distance. But even if A is a world military power, a small State B may be substantially invulnerable to its military force either because the coercive exercise of such force is too costly to A when considering the broad range of possible conflicts of interest and/or because B can count on support from a militarily powerful ally.

This consideration brings us to the second mechanism through which a state's military power may become effective in affecting another's behavior, namely the use of a military threat. Assuming a severe conflict between A and B, and assuming furthermore that all other means of influence have been exhausted, the effectiveness of a military threat by A against B would depend upon:

1. The estimate of B's government of

a. the balance of interests at stake, *i.e.,* the disutility of the threatened action compared with the disutility of compliance,

b. the probability that A will proceed to execute its threat in the event of noncompliance,

c. the character of domestic and foreign support for alternative courses of action.

2. The skill of A's and B's governments in the bargaining process.

3. The propensity of B's government to accept military risks and to behave rationally.

This list of factors specifies the conditions under which the effectiveness of A's threat, and hence the actualization of its power, will vary from total to zero. The first of these is self-explanatory. The second may be important since specific military threats are usually made in the course of an intense diplomatic confrontation; within this crisis context, the effectiveness of a military threat depends to some extent on its timing, nature of delivery and similar characteristics which can be chosen with greater or lesser skill. Similarly, the way in which a threat is received, and the response to it in terms of procrastination, evasiveness, appeals for reconsideration, or counter-threats may affect its success. The choice of such responses is also subject to the skill of leadership.[3] In regard to the third condition listed, the propensity to accept military risks and to approach crisis situations rationally are important since government and military leaders differ in these respects.[4] Some leaders have a stronger propensity to act rationally than others, and some are more inclined than others to run risks.

This model, as all models in this chapter, could be made more complex by differentiating various sub-variables for each of the listed factors. For example, B's estimates of relevant conditions depend on its power of perception, that is, the accuracy of its information and its ability to interpret this information. B's estimate of the probability that A will execute its threat depends on B's perceptions of the military means available to A for executing the threat, on the support A is likely to receive at home and abroad, and on A's previous record of resorting to force.

In turn, the willingness of A's government to make a military threat against B depends chiefly on the following factors:

1. The estimate of A's government of

a. the value of the gains it hopes to obtain from the threat compared with the costs of making the threat,

---

[3] The element of skill tends to rise in importance if we relax our simplifying assumption that means of influence other than military coercion have been exhausted. If, as is usually the case, other means of influence, whether noncoercive or coercive, continue to be available to the contending governments, then skill in concerting their employment carries especial weight in the outcome of military threats.

[4] Donald L. Harnett, Larry L. Cummings, and G. David Hughes, "The Influence of Risk-Taking Propensity on Bargaining Behavior," *Behavioral Science*, XIII (1968), pp. 91–101.

b. the effectiveness of the threat on B,

c. the strength of nature of domestic and foreign support of, or opposition to, the threat.

2. A's propensity to accept military risks and behave rationally.

This list of factors specifies the conditions under which A's willingness to resort to a military threat will range from extremely high to zero. The list could be greatly lengthened by differentiating between different gains and costs. Thus, the gains which State A hopes to secure involve the issue or issues at stake in the conflict with B that gave rise to the considered use of coercive power. But as soon as A resorts to a military threat, other values may come into play, for example, the immediate value of giving confidence to an ally. They may also include more diffuse future benefits resulting from a reputation for the forthright or cautious use of military power. If we focus on A as a particular government or regime, rather than as a state acting through a government, the gains may involve an increase in domestic power or other such benefits, including perhaps personal glory, to which its leaders may be attracted.

On the other side, the costs of employing a military threat may also touch on many different values. Among these costs, as perceived and evaluated by A's government, may be unfavorable domestic and foreign responses. If a threat is widely held to be clumsy, a nation's or a government's reputation for finesse may decline. If a threat is widely regarded as unjust or brutal, their moral reputation may suffer. For example, by the 1960's, and even earlier, the expectation of such costs tended to inhibit nuclear powers from employing their nuclear arms against a state without such weapons. A military threat may be illegal under the UN charter and provoke UN action because it is regarded as a threat to peace. In addition, a threat may lead to counterthreats by third states. One possible cost of a threat is that it may be defied. The very act of defiance may do damage to the threatening state's reputation as a powerful country. And if the threat is defied, there are also the costs of either making good the threat, including the costs and risks of war and foreign intervention, or the costs, in terms of reputation, of having one's bluff called.

It follows from our model that actualized military power is usually dependent on asymmetries in the costs of making threats and in the values at stake, as estimated by the two disputing governments, and in the prospect of foreign military support. This holds true when, as is often the case, there are small or no differences in the propensity to accept risks or behave rationally. The values at stake, the costs of making a threat, and the prospects of support from third states are more likely to vary. For instance, it is consistent with the above model that a State B may take a military threat against a State A which possesses substantially greater putative military power, and this not because B's leaders are irrational or have an extremely high propensity to accept military risks. They may do so, of course, in the event they have effective military backing from a third power with which A is reluctant to tangle; but they may also do so because the issue at stake, perhaps only moderately important to A, is absolutely vital to B; and it is possible that some of the costs of using a military threat—for example, domestic and foreign criticism—are smaller for the weaker than for the stronger military power.

Turning to war as a mechanism through which A's instrumental military power may affect B's behavior, the outcome will normally be decided by the decisions of the two governments to continue or to terminate hostilities at various stages of the conflict. For both governments, the main considerations will be their estimates of:

1. the military prospects of victory, stalemate or defeat,

2. the value of the stakes involved (which, however, may differ appreciably from those that led to crisis and war),

3. the various costs of inflicting and suffering further military violence,

4. the strength of domestic and foreign support, and the possibility of foreign intervention on either side.

5. the other party's evaluation of these conditions.

Again, these factors determine State A's actualized military power over B which, making allowance for B's actualized counter-power over A, is a net effect in terms of influence. It is obvious that the sooner B offers to terminate the war, and the more willing it is to do so on A's terms, the greater is A's actualized military power. But this analysis makes it clear that the terms of conflict settlement do not reflect merely the balance of tested military strength between A and B. It calls attention to other variable factors in the equation. Certainly actual military power does not result only from the possession of military forces, or a superiority in such capabilities; it also results from the will to put these forces, or this superiority, to use. In other words, it is crucially the result of purpose, determined by the stakes of the conflict, and of readiness to bear the various costs of employing force, including the risk of intervention by other states. The equation, which could be further complicated by the introduction of sub-variables, shows, furthermore, that to measure actualized military power in the concrete instance would be a formidable and, as it seems safe to conclude in most cases, a prohibitive task.

It is clear from the foregoing that the transformation of putative military power into actualized power is subject to several variable conditions. It is also clear that, depending on the concatenation of these conditions, the transformation of putative into actualized power may be great or small, and under some extreme circumstances may even approach zero. Nevertheless, other factors remaining the same, actualized or actualizable military power will be the greater, the more potent is a state's putative power.

Changes in Power Gains and Costs

In applying the model we have developed, it is interesting to note that the gains a state may obtain by employing military power are subject to modification over time as the governing criteria for evaluating such gains change. It is observable, for instance, that the traditional attraction of territorial conquest has waned in recent decades, particularly for the technologically more advanced nations. This has happened largely, though not only, because alternative avenues to increased wealth and power have been recognized as more productive.[5]

Even more conspicuous has been an increase in the costs of using military force.[6] This change has occurred partly because standards of valuation have changed; for example, the individual's welfare counts for more than it used to count in many societies, and his sacrifice is therefore held justified only if the nation's stakes are very high. Partly, the increase in costs has occurred because the aggressive use of military power has lost legitimacy, as is evidenced in the United Nations Charter. And, in part, costs have mounted because modern military technology has supplied nuclear weapons capable of inflicting unprecedentedly massive destruction against which there is thus far no adequate defense. This condition has rendered war between nuclear powers too costly for virtually any conceivable purpose. This does not mean that such military power has become useless. On the contrary, it is the threat of inflicting such unprecedented damage on an opponent which surely acts as a coercive means of influence and deters any adversary from launching an attack, or even from bringing about conflicts which might escalate to the strategic nuclear level. Moreover, when intense crises occur between nuclear powers, bargaining moves which increase the risk of nuclear war—a risk in which both parties share—are employed deliberately in order to secure a relatively favorable outcome of the crisis. As has been observed, these contests have become less a contest of military strength—of which at present each great nuclear power possesses enough to devastate the homeland of the other, even if attacked first—than a contest of nerve and will.[7] As we have seen above, the outcome of such a contest depends mainly on the values at stake to each opponent, and on their propensity to accept military risks and to act rationally.

Nevertheless, the rise in the costs of employing military power means that its usability has declined recently, especially for the great military powers; and this decline tends to diminish its utility. Furthermore, in examining the uses of military power, a distinction can be made between the purpose of deterrence and the purpose of "compellence."[8] Both are coercive uses of military power, but deterrence employs a threat in order to keep an opponent from doing something he might otherwise be tempted to do , while compellence employs a threat in order to make him do something which he would otherwise not choose to do. Given this distinction, it may be observed

---

[5] *Cf.* Klaus Knorr, *On the Uses of Military Power in the Nuclear Age,* (Princeton: Princeton University Press, 1966), Ch. II.

[6] *Ibid., passim.*

[7] *Cf.* Schelling, *Arms and Influence,* Ch. II.

[8] *Ibid.,* pp. 69ff.

that the rising costs of employing military power has caused the usability of force for compellence to decline more than for deterrence.

To complete this part of the analysis, the use of putative military power simply for the purpose of taking or holding an object of interstate contention by sheer force, a use of force involving no attempt to influence an opponent, depends upon a more limited set of conditions than those indicated in connection with military coercion. In order to make use of military power for this purpose, a state must have the required capabilities and the will to use them, and this positive will is determined by the net balance of prospective gains over cost and the propensity to accept military risks and act rationally. The effectiveness of military power in this kind of application is governed by the relationship of the opposing military forces in the theater of war, and the relationship between each side's will to fight and to continue fighting; this latter relationship, in turn, depends in part on each government's estimate of the other's will to continue the war. Of course, both the will to fight and the outcome are also subject to the intervention, actual or threatened, on the part of third states. Furthermore, the disposition of states to use force for this purpose is conditioned by the kinds of changes in the valuation of gains, and in the costs of resorting to military power, which were discussed above.

Statesmen think in terms of both putative and actualized military power even though they do not use these terms. If they are concerned with the employment of military power in the course of crisis bargaining, they will necessarily consider the conditions, prospects and consequences of its effectiveness in particular situations. Their perceptions of such power situations may be awry, and their ability to predict may be unreliable; but they will be compelled to consider the variable conditions which may determine the outcome of an international conflict.

Military Power Rankings

When not concerned with a serious international crisis, statesmen will nevertheless be aware of international relationships of influence including those of military power. This awareness produces a ranking of states in terms of military power, that is, in terms of the military power which, though putative, may nevertheless influence state behavior through the anticipation of the use of force. If some states are ranked as great powers, this means that there is an expectation, widely distributed throughout the international system, that these states are (a) capable, within a broad range of international conflict situations, of bringing military force to bear; and (b) willing, with some degree of probability, to do so if they deem the stakes to be sufficiently high in relation to the costs of resorting to military force. Usually such states also have, as mentioned earlier, a high and recognized propensity to use force internationally. This basic propensity may be defined as a settled sensitivity, developed over time, to the advantages of using force internationally, and a settled insensitivity to some of the disadvantages, including moral disadvantages, of appealing to force.

Comparatively speaking, middle and small military powers are recognized to lack, in some of these factors. A lesser power may have a very high basic propensity to resort to force, but a deficiency in the resources needed to produce substantial military forces either in terms of size or of effective equipment. Yet it is also possible that a state may be a lesser power, not because it lacks the wealth to produce large military forces, but because it chooses to maintain smaller forces than do countries of comparable size and resources, or perhaps because its propensity to employ military power is low.

It was fairly easy to rank the nations of Europe in terms of military power from the seventeenth through the nineteenth century.[9] But it has become much more difficult in recent decades, especially since World War II, to make such comparisons. Three major conditions largely account for this change.

First, as pointed out above, the usability of military power has decreased largely because the costs of using force have risen, and this development alone has made the probability that a nation will employ military power smaller and more contingent. Moreover, the diminished legitimacy of war has lessened the probability that a militarily weak country will yield to the military threat of a superior state; and the fact that the governments of superior states realize this tends to inhibit a forthright appeal to arms.

Second, military forces have lost versatility in terms of the kinds of conflict that arise in the contemporary world. Several conditions have brought about this result. (a) A strategic nuclear capability may have great value for purposes of deterring a nuclear power, but it has practically no value for purposes of compellence, unless the compelling power is so superior that it is able to disarm the other nuclear state by striking first. Deterrence, moreover, though of course requiring the requisite nuclear armament, rests heavily on the credibility of the retaliatory threat—that is to say, on will, nerve, and commitment—and these conditions are apt to be highly changeable with reference to the stakes involved in an interstate dispute. Further, the danger that armed conflict may escalate to the nuclear level increases the risk of a resort to conventional force between nuclear powers, and thus leads to some discount of force differences in the conventional category. Finally, the worldwide horror of nuclear explosives has generated the attachment of a powerful stigma to their use and strongly inhibits their employment especially against non-nuclear states—another example of the increase in the costs of using

---

[9] For some of the reasons which made this more difficult before the seventeenth century, see Robert E. Osgood and Robert W. Tucker, *Force, Order, and Justice* (Baltimore: Johns Hopkins University Press, 1967), Pt. I. Ch. 2.

military force. (b) For states which have developed nuclear military forces, the expense of producing nuclear capabilities has reduced their ability, especially, the ability of the middle powers, to maintain sizeable conventional capabilities, and particualy conventional forces capable of operating at any considerable distance from the home base. (c) The present age of revolutionary violence has witnessed the rising importance of what has been inelegantly called "sub-limited war" and "counterinsurgency war," that is, the military intervention or counterintervention in civil wars, as the United Stated did in South Vietnam in the 1960's. As is true of the antagonists in classical warfare, the aim of insurgents and counterinsurgents is to take or defend by sheer force and to erode the enemy's will to fight. But in this type of conflict, a political contest aimed at increasing support by the local population usually dominates the military struggle; besides, since the military operations usually involve actions against guerrillas and terrorists, often in areas with difficult and poor means of communication, the capabilities required are very different from those demanded for nuclear or conventional war. Even a great power may have quite unsuitable capabilities, military and political, for such intervention though it may be superbly equipped for nuclear or conventional warfare.

Third, the global distribution of power since World War II has been largely bipolar, though decreasingly so in the 1960's. A consequence of this pattern is that either of the two super-powers, when contemplating the use of military power against another state, must reckon with the intervention of the other great power. This probability has risen as a result of the ramified alliance commitments made by these states, and of their ceaseless competition for the allegiances of uncommitted countries. This prospect naturally inhibits resort to military power unless the purposes are very compelling.

These conditions combine to make it more difficult than it once was to rank states in terms of military power; they also make ranking less meaningful. Indeed, they are conditions which variously restrict the possibility that the possession of military forces becomes productive of military power. The actualization of putative power has become more difficult, and such power has lost in value.

However, it would be unwise to go too far and deny any usefulness to power rankings, or to rush to the conclusion that military power has become irrelevant, or even to assume that its significance has shrunk to a small fraction of its former value. Such an inference is certainly not borne out by the crises over Berlin, the Korean War, the Cuban Missile Crisis, the war in Vietnam, the Arab-Israeli War of 1967, the Greco-Turkish crisis over Cyprus in the same year, and other recent conflicts of this kind. The abundant efforts of governments the world over to establish or maintain sizeable armed forces testifies to the continued importance attributed to military power, however conditional such power may have become in recent decades.

Functions

Viewed from the perspective of individual nation-states, the function of military power, like that of other types of influence, is to advance or defend vital national interests of the arena in international competition for scarce values—such as territory, security and international leadership—especially if their advancement or defense by other means proves frustrating. Viewed from the perspective of the international system of all states, military power has been said to provide a basis for international order. Indeed, it is claimed that there is no substitute for this basis of order; in the absence of a higher, supranational authority with effective legal power, the settlement of international disputes must rest on national military power whenever other means of influence fail to produce a satisfactory resolution and the non-resolution of conflict is intolerable. Whether or not truth is attributed to this claim, or to the opposite claim that the prevailing international system is one of anarchy, depends on one's criteria for judgment.

National military power generates international order in the sense that the freedom of states to act internationally is restrained by the expected disutilities of appealing to, or provoking, the use of military force. This restraint operates not only on states that are militarily weak, but also on those which are militarily powerful, although with lesser weight. And it is important to note in this connection that many states which are weak *vis-à-vis* some states are strong *vis-a-vis* others. There are several effective restraints to which the militarily superior state is subject in the use of force: the risk of stimulating the formation of a hostile, perhaps stronger, coalition of states, the various risks and other costs of war itself, and legal and moral sanctions.

Nevertheless, international order which rests on the distribution of national military power is deficient in several respects. As the history of war demonstrates impressively, such an order has not proved to be a very stable one, although the degree of instability has fluctuated over time. The many tests to which it has been put have caused enormous suffering and destruction. To the extent that this order works, it cannot help but favor the militarily stronger countries; and unless one believes that "might makes right," one sees no tested or even logically plausible evidence that the international distribution of national military power has anything but a random relationship with the distribution of justice. Of course, the costs of maintaining this form of order must be compared with the probable costs of employing any alternative form.

2 The Concept of Military Potential

The military potential of states is one of the bases of military power. This potential is equal to the national resources available for producing and maintaining armed forces. Whenever a nation creates or expands military forces in peace or war, it mobilizes military potential. The concept is concerned with an input-output relationship. Available and suitable resources are the input; military forces, or strength, are the output.

Although the focus of this chapter is on national military potential as preliminarily defined—that is, on factors available for *producing* military strength—it will also be concerned throughout with national potential for *employing* military strength, since many of the factors determining the one potential also determine the other.

Potential for What?

The study of military potential is a kind of capability analysis. As has been rightly observed, capabilities can be sensibly estimated only with reference to particular objectives, strategies and contingencies.[1] The relevant questions are: what is to be accomplished, by which courses of action, and under what circumstances? Throughout this study the reader should keep in mind this element of conditionality in

---

[1] *Cf.* Harold and Margaret Sprout, *An Ecological Paradigm for the Study of International Politics,* Princeton University, Center of International Studies, Research Monograph No. 30 (1968), p. 35.

the evaluation of military potential. However, this does not mean that goals, strategies and contingencies must be precisely predicted prior to utilizing capability analysis. Planners of foreign and military policy would be paralyzed if this were so. In fact, there are types of objectives, strategies and contingencies which can be analyzed and projected. Furthermore, the observed relationship is reciprocal. It is not only that capabilities are meaningful merely with reference to objectives, strategies and operational conditions. National capabilities also have a bearing on the choice of objectives and strategies, and through these choices they influence the probability with which some contingencies will arise. Certainly, historical experience with contests of military forces makes it plain that future contingencies are not predictable with any degree of confidence. It is nevertheless possible and useful to conjecture about kinds of contingencies.[2] Indeed, in view of the inevitable intrusion of uncertainties about the future, their rational consideration and the provision for flexibility is an important part of overall capability. Finally, when putative military power becomes actualized through the third mechanism discussed in Chapter I, the relatedness of capabilities on the one side and objectives, strategies and contingencies on the other is extremely loose.

A Historical Note on "War Potential"

During the latter part of the nineteenth century, concern with military potential was focused on the narrower concept of *war potential;* this concept remained in use through World War II and continues in more limited use up to the present time. As the words imply, the concept concerns economic resources available for mobilization in time of war. It was important especially during the sixty-year period from the 1880's to the 1940's, after industrialization had begun greatly to increase the productive power of the technologically more advanced nations. During this period states did not normally maintain in peacetime the size of military forces which they were capable of mobilizing in wartime. For example, in 1939, Germany produced only 20 percent of the volume of combat munitions which it manufactured in 1944. Similarly, the United Kingdom turned out in 1940 one third of the combat munitions it was to produce in 1944; and the United States and Japan produced as late as 1942 a mere half of their munitions output in 1944.[3]

In peacetime, nations naturally preferred to limit military expenditures in order to employ more resources for consumption and investment; and they were able to do so for two reasons. First, they all

[2]*Cf.* Klaus Knorr and Oskar Morgenstern, *Political Conjecture in Military Planning,* Princeton University, Center of International Studies, Policy Memorandum No. 35 (1968).
[3]R.W. Goldsmith, "The Power of Victory: Munitions Output in World War II," *Military Affairs,* X (1946), p. 72.

adhered to the same practice, which reduced the risk of insufficient mobilization for any single nation. To be sure, occasional arms races would lead to an additional mobilization of resources, but even then outlays on military strength stayed usually far short of the level feasible in time of war. Second, nations could usually afford to follow this practice without assuming undue risk because, given the state of military technology during these sixty years, governments could count on ample time for the mobilization of potential strength. This process often began when severe international crises occurred, and it could be completed after the outbreak of hostilities as long as the ready military forces on hand could prevent a quick military decision favoring the opponent. Under these circumstances, when statesmen resorted to estimates of military power, as they were often forced to do in the pursuit of foreign policy, or when military staffs prepared war plans for likely contingencies, they obviously had to reckon with more than the national military forces on hand. War potential could not be neglected. It was recognized to be part of a state's military power.

War potential played a crucial part in the outcomes of World Wars I and II, for these were essentially wars of attrition. In both instances, the coalition with inferior manpower and industrial capacity lost to the coalition with superior resources. Indeed, World War II is especially interesting in this respect since Germany, having mobilized before the war substantially more resources than its future enemies, began hostilities with a considerable advantage. From 1935 to 1939, the volume of combat munitions (measured in U.S. dollars at 1944 munitions prices) produced by the main countries was: Germany $12.0 billion, Soviet Russia $8.0 billion, Britain $2.5 billion, Japan $2.0 billion, and the United States $1.5 billion.[4] Since war is fought on the basis of accumulated as well as currently produced munitions, Germany had clearly a great advantage at the outset, and this fact may account in part for her early victories. Table 1 shows how this condition changed in the course of the war. While in 1939 the Axis countries still accounted for 55 percent of the total output of combat munitions, four years later their share had dropped to 30 percent. In that year, the United States alone outproduced Germany, Italy and Japan together by a third. This gradual change in munitions production parallels closely the changing turn in the fortunes of war.

These data suggest the overwhelming weight of massive manpower and war supplies on the battlefields of World War II. There were certainly other factors, differences in leadership, morale, and the quality of weapons and other supplies, that decisively affected the outcome of battles and campaigns. But taken together these other factors did not seem to have dominated the war as a whole. The gradual buildup of a preponderance in materiel, as well as greater reserves of manpower, appear to have been decisive in the end.

[4] *Ibid.*, p. 71.

TABLE 1
Combat Munitions[a] Output of the Main Belligerents, 1938–1943[5] (percentage of total)

Country	1938	1939	1940	1941	1942	1943
United States	6	4	7	14	30	40
Canada	0	0	0	1	2	2
Britain	6	10	18	19	15	13
USSR	27	31	23	24	17	15
TOTAL, United Nations	39	45	48	58	64	70
Germany[b]	46	43	40	31	27	22
Italy	6	4	5	4	3	1
Japan	9	8	7	7	6	7
TOTAL, Axis Countries	61	55	52	42	36	30
GRAND TOTAL	100	100	100	100	100	100

[a]Includes aircraft, army ground ordnance and signal equipment, naval vessels, and related equipment.
[b]Includes occupied territories.

This pattern of cause and result had also been true of World War I and of the American Civil War. War potential was no doubt important, though no doubt varyingly, in the prolonged wars of preceding periods. But it is plausible to assume that the great wars of attrition between the middle of the eighteenth and the middle of the nineteenth century reflected the increasing, though uneven, industrialization and wealth of the belligerent powers. Advancing technology and industrial production greatly raised the production capacity of the states engaged in rapid economic development. This progress made it possible for them, when they chose, in an emergency, to free an ever larger proportion of their resources from producing for current consumption and investment, and to allocate the "surplus" to the military sector of society. This change in the war potential of the industrialized countries had not in fact been fully understood by their

[5]Adapted from U.S. War Production Board, Bureau of Planning and Statistics, *World Munitions Production, 1938–1944*, (mimeographed) Document No. 21 (Washington, D.C., July 15, 1944), p. 33. This tabulation presents only a very rough comparison of magnitudes. In the absence of adequate quantitative data on various munitions produced, the table contains estimates based on domestic military expenditures, approximately adjusted for non-munitions expenditures and for differences in the price levels of munitions, and checked, so far as possible, against available figures on the physical volume of output. These adjusted data for total expenditures on combat munitions were all expressed in U.S. dollars at current or prewar rates of exchange. Since these exchange rates overvalued or undervalued, to varying extents, one currency in terms of others, the obtained computations are subject to error. It can be assumed, however, that the errors are marginal and that the presented data do not grossly falsify actual output trends and magnitudes.

leaders before World War I had run half its course.[6] Only then did they realize that warfare had become a highly industrialized activity, and that the capacity to produce abundantly had become the crucial basis of national military power.

Shortly after the events of World War II had strikingly emphasized the importance of war potential, and particularly industrial war potential, as a base of military strength, the advent of the nuclear bomb led many observers to question, if not deny outright, the future usefulness of the concept. Since a small number of nuclear bombs could cripple, if not completely destroy, any country, and since no effective defense existed against delivery vehicles, it was inferred that a war between nuclear powers, or perhaps even a war involving one nuclear power, would be over in a matter of days or weeks. Obviously there would be no time for nations to mobilize their war potential once nuclear war had broken out. All that counted, therefore, were nuclear forces entirely ready in time of peace in order to deter a hostile strike, including a surprise attack. It was inferred, furthermore, that even if nuclear powers chose not to resort immediately to their nuclear strategic armaments in the event of conventional hostilities, these could only be very limited hostilities (e.g., border skirmishes, military encounters in third countries), and of short duration. It seemed unimaginable that powers in possession of nuclear forces would engage in a protracted war of attrition on the scale of World War I or II. For these reasons, it seemed war potential had become irrelevant.

Today, these inferences, though they remain valid in large part, require considerable qualification. There can be no doubt that war potential is of little, if any, consequence in the event of a large-scale nuclear war between opponents each of which is able to obliterate the major urban and industrial centers of the other, or one of which is superior enough to disarm the other by a first strike. In either case, the strategic forces that would be used would be those operationally in being at the beginning of the war. The Soviet strategic literature[7] makes much of a hypothetical war phase, following an initial nuclear exchange, in which surface forces equipped with conventional as well as tacticalnuclear arms would continue to fight, presumably offensively as well as defensively. The American literature has paid little attention to this "broken-back" phase of a major war between nuclear powers. In any case, this phase would seem to involve predominantly, if not exclusively, forces and materiel on hand at the start of hostilities.

Nevertheless, the thesis that war potential has become obsolete has only limited application. First, there are many non-nuclear states

[6]Cf. Klaus Knorr, *The War Potential of Nations* (Princeton: Princeton University Press, 1963), esp. Chs. IV–VII.
[7]Cf. Marshall V.D. Sokolovsky, *Military Strategy* (New York: Frederick A. Praeger, 1963), esp. Chs. IV–VIII.

capable of waging war among themselves, and for them war potential has not, in principle, lost significance even though the wars between such states since World War II have actually been short or limited, or both (e.g., the border war between China and India in 1962, the war between India and Pakistan in 1965, the fighting between Indonesia and Malaysia in 1963–66, and the Israeli-Arab war of 1967). Surely, Arab leaders are interested in Israel's war potential, and vise versa.

Second, there can be sizable conventional wars between a nuclear power and a non-nuclear one. This happened in the Korean War and in American fighting in South Vietnam and, in the air, against North Vietnam. The United States was unable to fight either war with forces and equipment in being at the outset; it proceeded to considerable mobilization of war potential although not, of course, to the degree required in World War II.[8] As mentioned in Chapter I, a widely diffused revulsion to nuclear weapons has attached a powerful stigma to their employment; the resulting expectation of opprobrium will keep any nuclear-weapon states from using these arms against a non-nuclear opponent, except perhaps under the most challenging circumstances, and even then presumably with great restraint. It seems conceivable, therefore, that a nuclear power could become involved in large-scale and protracted warfare against a non-nuclear state.

Finally, even as far as possible military confrontation between the great powers is concerned, there have been changes in the strategic assumptions and policies of the 1950's. Thus, the doctrine of flexible response, enunciated by the United States government in the early 1960's,[9] attempted to provide a substantial conventional option to immediate resort to a strategic nuclear threat in the event fighting between Communist and NATO forces broke out in central Europe. The United States government set out to persuade its NATO allies to support a plan envisioning the deployment of more than 30 full divisions, and also requiring considerable reserves. The assumption underlying this strategy contemplated rather large-scale fighting for an appreciable period of time, a contingency which would almost certainly be associated with considerable mobilization. Yet this is a contingency which taxes one's imagination severely. A large and prolonged war between the United States and the Soviet Union, and their allies, is extremely improbable as long as mutual deterrence prevails on the strategic nuclear level. The governments concerned could hardly take lightly the enormous risk that a serious war between them could stay limited and not escalate, if only by inadvertence or

---

[8]Thus, the national security expenditures of the United States mounted from $18.5 billion in 1950 to $37.3 billion in 1951, and $48.8 billion in 1952. Similarly, the armed forces expanded from 1,650,000 men in 1950 to 3,098,000 in 1951 and 3,594,000 in 1952. Defense expenditures, which had amounted to about $50 billion a year in 1962–65, rose to $60.5 billion in 1966, and $72.6 billion in 1967.

[9]Cf. William W. Kaufmann, *The McNamara Strategy* (New York: Harper & Row, 1964), Chs. II–III.

accident, to the level that would bring unacceptable destruction to all countries involved.

Military Potential Versus War Potential

In any case, in appreciating the phenomenon of military power, it is not the limited concept of *war* potential, but the broader concept of *military* potential which is indispensable, and this concept has lost none of its significance on account of the new military technology. Nations differ greatly at all times in the resource base which they could mobilize to varying degrees in order to produce and maintain the armed services on which military power in large part rests. Viewed from this perspective, the dividing line between formal peace and war becomes immaterial except insofar as nations may, at a time of sharp diplomatic crisis, or engaged in an arms race with another power or powers, or in time of war, increase the rate of mobilization. Whether a state can afford to develop and deploy nuclear capabilities for the purpose of deterring any nuclear opponent at all times, and what magnitude and kind of such forces it can afford, depends upon its military potential. So does the generation of all other types of military capabilities: for tactical nuclear war, for conventional war, or for armed intervention in the civil strife of other countries. Moreover, the significance of military potential is not confined to the production of the national military forces of the state concerned. It also affects its ability to export arms and military instruction to allies and other countries. In 1967–68, when the military potential of the United States was in part mobilized for conducting war in Vietnam, the Soviet potential was taxed for sending a large volume of arms to North Vietnam to be used in its fighting against the United States, and to the Arab states whose inventory had been depleted by Israeli military action. In large part and indispensably, nations become military powers of consequence, globally or within a region, because they have a superior military potential, which even with a moderate rate of mobilization generates commanding ready military strength, or because, though endowed with a moderate potential in terms of manpower and other resources in terms of manpower and other resources, they mobilize to a greater extent than do states of comparable military potential.

Military potential has a bearing on a nation's putative military power. This power, as we have seen in Chapter I, results from ready military forces, from the ability to augment these forces, and from a nation's reputation for employing military force in the event of a serious international dispute. The first two factors—ready, mobilized forces and military potential—may be regarded as a nation's military strength which figures in the equation of putative military power. Indeed, military potential may be a factor even in actualized military power. Although battles can be won only with mobilized strength— many a state has lost a war because it failed to mobilize more of its potential strength in time—the expectation of a belligerent that its adversary can mobilize further resources for future battles may influence his decision to terminate a military conflict on tolerable terms.

The Sinews of Military Strength

In practice, the concept of military potential has been employed mostly with reference to *economic* potential. This focus is not surprising for two reasons. First, as will be demonstrated below, it is much easier to study, measure and compare economic military potential than political, administrative and psychological factors that have a bearing on the amount of military strength a nation-state can generate. Second, the concept of potential acquired considerable currency *after* World War I, and the statesmen, soldiers and scholars of this period were deeply impressed by what we have called the "industrialization" of warfare, that is, by the critical importance of industrially produced equipment in the fighting ability of modern military forces. However, the observed fact that the nations with the superior supply of manpower and industrial capacity vanquished their enemies in World Wars I and II does not prove that these two factors will prove equally decisive in any future wars, and especially not in wars of a type quite different from these two prolonged wars of attrition. Nor is economic potential crucial in brief conflicts, or in encounters which, though prolonged, do not involve men and materiel in large numbers, or in routine peacetime maintenance of armed forces at a modest level to which a nation has become adjusted. The importance of economic potential is proportional to the demands on economic resources made by military exigencies.

In order to elucidate the problem of comparing the military potential of states, one may begin by noting the difficulties encountered in comparing their *mobilized* military strength, that is, in comparing their combat power. There are neither theoretical guidance nor empirical apparatus for measuring and comparing, and essentially predicting, the combat strength of the mobilized forces of different states.[10] The only known measurement test which is accurate is the test of battle. Of course, quantitative comparisons of infantry divisions, aircraft wings, naval vessels, missile launchers and military personnel can be made. *The Military Balance* published each year by the Institute for Strategic Studies in London provides much of the data, and more of this kind of information can be assembled from other public sources. But if we had taken *The Military Balance, 1966–67,* and studied the fairly detailed entries on the armed services of Israel and the United Arab Republic, we would have noted an

[10]This does not mean that military intelligence services are not busy to undertake such comparisons. But this involves a great deal of guesswork. The results are more or less impressionistic and justify only low confidence.

appreciable degree of U.A.R. superiority (*e.g.,* about 550 military aircraft for the U.A.R. versus 350 for Israel). Such a comparison would have left us completely unprepared for the outcome of the Israeli-Arab war in 1967, which was determined largely, and probably decisively, by Israel's surprise air strike which destroyed the bulk of the U.A.R.'s airpower on the ground. Every war knows its surprises and is conditioned by special circumstances that render it more or less unique. But the main problem arises from the fact that the presence of qualitative factors makes quantitative comparisons often inconclusive. In the Israeli-Arab war, important qualitative differences, in addition to the sweeping air superiority gained by an audacious surprise attack, were superior Israeli tactics especially in the use of armored motorized forces, facilitated by great speed of movement at night as well as by day, superior communication of commands, superior skill of the Israeli soldier in operating complicated equipment—especially superb gunnery from aircraft, tanks and artillery—and also the superior morale and élan of Israeli forces, which were basically a citizen's army fired by the knowledge that it was fighting for national survival.[11] This broad intrusion of qualitative differences is not at all unusual. It would have been equally difficult to compare, before the event, the fighting strength of North Vietnamese regulars and U.S. marines south of the Demilitarized Zone along the Seventeenth Parallel.

The main qualitative differences result from the following factors: (1) different composition of national forces as among (and within) the army, navy, air force and various special forces; (2) different composition and qualitative differences of weaponry and other military materiel; (3) differences in military strategy, doctrine, tactics and other components of military leadership; (4) differences in military communications and control systems; (5) differences in military intelligence; and (6) differences in troops in terms of skill and training, physical stamina, ability to endure various deprivations, morale, valor, etc.

Even if we assume that superior industrial capacity is mobilized for generating combat power and reflects itself in qualitative as well as quantitative superiority of weapons (which is not a necessary inference) and in superior skill and discipline associated with their use, marked deficiencies in other qualitative factors might still eventuate in inferior combat power. We do not have sufficient knowledge for suggesting exact and invariable relationships between these several factors, so that it would become apparent how much superiority in some factors would offset how much inferiority in others; nor are many of the qualitative factors tangible enough to allow measurement. But there are numerous historical examples which caution against

[11]*Cv.* General Beaufre, "Une guerre classique moderne: la guerre israelo-arabe," and "Les enseignements operationnels de la guerre israelo-arabe," *Strategie* (Paris, Institut Francais d'Etudes Stategiques), No. 13 (1967), pp. 7–25, 27–36; Brigadier General S.L.A. Marshal, "The Army of Israel," *Military Review,* April 1968, pp. 3–9.

accepting the power of sheer numbers. To cite one example from World War II, the German conquest of France was achieved despite the fact that the Germans were inferior in numbers of men and tanks, though superior in aircraft. They won by dint of strategic surprise (*e.g.,* invasion through an area suspected to be virtually impenetrable by armored forces), by superior tactics and probably also by superior morale.[12] According to historical evidence about many battles and wars, the margin of superiority may be provided by various combinations of the constituents of mobilized strength, quantitative or qualitative. It is fair to assume that this holds true in the present of all kinds of war, whether counterinsurgent or conventional. Even the outcome of strategic nuclear war, should it ever occur, would not escape the effect of many variable determinants. There are differences not only in numbers of strategic nuclear weapons, but also in their range, explosive yield, accuracy, reliability and vulnerability, in the efficacy of command-and-control systems, in target systems, and in the human element commanding and manning these capabilities. Superior industrial capacity does not assure superiority in any of these properties even if it is a favorable condition in this respect.

Two recent developments have made qualitative differences more complex than they were before. One is the increasing technical complexity of particular weapons. Thus, modern aircraft carriers and fighter planes are much more complex machines than the battleships and military aircraft of World War II vintage; and there is no earlier counterpart to the intercontinental ballistic missile and its nuclear warhead. The other development parallels the increasing trend toward specialization observed in all technology. There are now many more specialized forces, weapons and gear than there were some decades ago. Both developments make for potentially large differences in qualitative performance.

The Components of Military Potential

The qualitative conditions of combat power result from factors which—to the extent that they do not originate in short-run or ephemeral conditions—belong properly to a nation's military potential; and so do a great many other conditions which are noneconomic and nontechnological, and are often hard to measure or unmeasurable. Morale and skill in blending the mix of weapons for various missions are obvious examples. The daunting fact is that there are few characteristics of a society which do or may not affect, directly or indirectly, its ability to generate and employ military power. Its

[12]*Cf.* L.F. Ellis, *The War in France and Flanders, 1939–1940,* History of the Second World War, United Kingdom Military Series, (London, H.M.S.O, 1953), *passim.*

political system, social structure and culture patterns are as relevant, though not necessarily as weighty, as its economic and technological resources and sheer numbers of population. Surely, political, social and cultural factors give Israel and the U.A.R. very different military potentials.

This broader approach to military potential is not meant to suggest that economic and technological factors and numbers of men are generally overrated as determinants of national military potential. The weight of these factors is undeniable. After all, in the late 1950's, all the states in the world together spent roughly $120 billion annually on military account, a figure equivalent to between 8 and 9 percent of world annual production of goods and services; and armed forces in the world numbered about 20 million persons.[13] The purpose of this discussion is only to draw attention to other important determinants of military potential.

Unfortunately, the present state of the social sciences does not permit a proper consideration and ordering of all these elements of national life that bear on a state's military potential. The obstacles stem from the facts that most of the social sciences have not progressed as far as economics has, that, regarding many aspects of social reality, available conceptualizations and empirical work have not been undertaken from the viewpoint relevant to the focus of this study, and that, though interesting information and hypotheses are scattered over the vast literatures of the social sciences and history, no one person commands enough expertise and time to gather these fragments together. These discouraging conditions force the present study to be more modest even though it will go far beyond analyzing economic war potential. This is a conceptual study which is meant to include what seem on intuitive grounds the most relevant constituents of national military potential. But little attention will be given to some factors, and some will be ignored altogether, especially those cultural conditions that impinge on such characteristics of military personnel as physical stamina, fortitude in the face of adversity, and military courage.

We distinguish between three broad categories of factors which together are largely determinant of a state's military potential. These are economic and technological capacity, administrative skill, and political foundations of military power.[14] These three components will be briefly described in the following paragraphs, and then more fully examined in separate chapters.

[13]United Nations, *Economic and Social Consequences of Disarmament* (New York, 1962), p. 3.
[14]In my earlier book *The War Potential of Nations,* I made the same distinctions but used somewhat different terms to refer to the three classes of factors. The terms preferred in the present study should prove less ambiguous than those employed in the earlier one. The structuring of factors within the categories is also different in the present book.

Economic and Technological Capacity

A nation's ability to mobilize and deploy military forces and supplies is determined in large part by its capacity to produce various goods and services, that is, by its labor force, raw materials, certain financial resources (*e.g.,* financial claims on foreigners); and the technical military effectiveness of its armed forces and supplies is also dependent on its technological resources. Mobilization in peace or war means that a proportion of these resources is diverted from other employment, or from idleness, to the production of ready military strength. Since a nation must subsist and carry on most of its non-military activities at all times, even in time of war, not all of this capacity is available for military purposes. But any military strength which is mobilized must be derived from this capacity except to the extent that a state is given military supplies, on credit or as a gift, from other states. Economic and technological capacity then depends on the size and structure of the population, that nation's territory with its land, water and mineral resources, the economic productivity of its labor force, its capital equipment, and the stage of its economic and technological development.

Administrative Skill

Administrative skill determines the efficiency with which economic and technological resources once diverted to the military sector are transformed into effective military forces. This transformation is a function of government and the military which must decide how manpower and equipment is to be combined in the armed services; it must decide on the composition of military output, that is, on the quantity, variety and quality of weapons and other materiel, and the size and structure of the armed forces themselves; it must decide on the training and indoctrination of military personnel, the development of military strategy, doctrine and tactics with reference to different contingencies, and all other conditions, subject to its control, which impinge on ready military strength. For example, a government, or its delegated military leaders, must choose the size of the army versus that of other armed services; their equipment; the number, kinds and deployment of nuclear arms (if a nuclear power is involved); the provision of military personnel with the necessities and amenities of life; the means of transporting troops to various possible theaters of war; the education of commanding and staff officers; and numerous other matters. Obviously, the more efficiently these decisions are made, the more military strength will be derived from any given allocation of men and other economic and technological resources. Moreover, not only is administrative skill important in converting economic and technological resources into mobilized strength of the right kind; it also determines the uses of this strength, efficiently or inefficiently, in time of peace or war.

Political Foundations of Military Power

Unlike economic and technological capacity, and administrative skill, which are readily understood and whose contribution to national military potential is immediately apparent, the political bases of military strength are less obvious and more difficult to identify and describe. Moreover, care must be taken in distinguishing between the determinants of potential military power and those factors which determine the mobilization of this potential; that is, *antecedent* conditions must be separated from *situational* factors.

The proportion of economic, technological, and administrative resources which a nation will actually allocate to producing military capabilities and the readiness with which it will support the international use of its military power depend upon a motivation—represented in its leadership and, to the extent it is politically effective, also in the rest of the population—which competes and sometimes conflicts with motivations to expend resources for other purposes, for instance consumption. The more strongly leaders and other groups are motivated to reduce or forego the satisfaction of interest and preferences that conflict with a large commitment to provide and employ military forces, the larger those forces and the greater the readiness to use them are likely to be.

This motivation to supply and apply military strength has several components and sources. Motivations favoring military power certainly depend upon the perceived need to resist military aggression or the perceived opportunities for employing military power aggressively, that is, on behalf of internationally acquisitive ends. The decision of a government to augment military forces or to use them, and the support of interested and influential publics depend clearly on perceptions and evaluations of the international situation existing at a particular time, and on cost-gain calculations concerning the usefulness of military power in that situation. Thus, the United States increased its military capabilities in the early 1950's when its government assumed that it faced the possibility of a powerful Soviet military challenge to the status of Berlin and the security of western Europe.

However, while a government's decision to increase military strength or to put it to international use is obviously governed by its reaction—and the reaction of other interested and politically influential groups—to the external situation, it is also influenced by various conditions prevailing in the political community of which it is the authoritative head. Its ability to increase military strength or to employ it internationally depends on public support, or perhaps even demands, expecially those from the politically influential public. This mobilizability of the nation depends in part, as already indicated, on the situational factors mentioned above, but it rests also on conditions which are antecedent to the external situation.

The public support potential depends mainly on four distinguishable antecedent factors. First, there is the nation's propensity to mobilize and use military power internationally. This is an attitude complex which favors more or less, or opposes more or less, military responses to international pressures and disputes. It is a predisposition which historians and other observers had in mind when they characterized tribes, cities, and states as more or less warlike or militaristic. In Chapter I we referred to this basic propensity as a settled sensitivity, developed as a result of historical experience, to some of the advantages of using force internationally, and a settled insensitivity to some of the disadvantages of doing so. Past experience creates a pattern of precedents influencing current behavior. Attitudes of this kind help to explain why Poland and Finland chose to fight overwhelmingly stronger states in 1939, whereas Czechoslovakia chose not to do so in 1938.

Second, there is the predisposition to support the national community. This attitude is based on a sense of solidarity, that is, an attachment which—notwithstanding political, social and cultural cleavages—ties citizens to a nation-state. This sense of national community is not specifically sensitive to military problems, but it tends to come strongly into play whenever a national emergency has been precipitated. If the emergency is of a military type, this disposition leads to demands for, and favors behavior toward, a "closing of ranks" in the face of danger, and the suspension of ordinary political partisanship. Even though the sense of community does not necessarily generate support for any military policy of the government, it is easily appealed to when the nation can be portrayed as facing external danger. The degree of solidarity prevailing in different states varies considerably even when cleavages are not deep. Moreover, if a deep cleavage—*i.e.,* along ethnic, language or cultural lines—has produced sharp political division, there may be a high level of solidarity in the state but two competing foci of solidarity may preclude a strong state-wide mobilization of support for this reason. The Austro-Hungarian monarchy just before World War I is a case in point. However, if the sense of community is undiminished by cleavages, and is strong, it will provide an especially copious basis for support when it is associated with a strong propensity to favor the use of military power internationally.

The third factor is the public disposition to support the foreign and military policy of the government or to accept it as authoritative and hence binding, on other grounds than the two attitudes already identified, and also on other grounds than the assessment by members of the public of the immediate external situation which poses the question of increasing or employing military strength. Such support can originate in a variety of motivations. Of these we single out two which seem to have been important historically and disregard a number of residual motivations which may be important in some particular situations but, on the basis of historical experience, cannot be said to have been important with any degree of frequency. One factor worth singling out is the public disposition to accept the government's foreign and military policies as authoritative either because all government policies tend to be thus accepted, or because foreign and military policy in particular is regarded by the public as involving matters in which the initiative of government is proper. The second factor relates not to government as an institution but to the qualities of leadership with which particular incumbents are endowed. The exercise of these qualities of leadership, involving public identification with the person of a leader, affects public support for government policy. Thus, Hitler and President de Gaulle found it much easier than their immediate predecessors to mobilize resources behind their countries' military effort.

The fourth factor is support for a government's foreign and military policy coming from members of the public because they have a direct and specific personal interest in the mobilization and use of military strength. This kind of support may greatly vary in scope. On the one hand, individuals and groups may be disposed to support increases and international uses of military strength regardless of the peculiarities of the external situation because they expect to derive pecuniary gains, career advantages or special psychological satisfactions. Thus there is the advantage to the military of large forces which benefit their career interests, satisfy their professional pride, redound to their prestige, or the advantage to business groups which derive benefits from large military expenditures. Whether the military or business groups are able to achieve an enlarged diversion of resources to the military sector depends, of course, on their political influence. On the other hand, there may be particular groups whose support is inspired in part by strong animosities against, or by strong ties of affinity and sympathy toward, a particular foreign state or foreign states. For example, American Jews were specially disposed to support the war against Nazi Germany in World War II and to back support of Israel against the Arab states after Israel had been established. This type of support also varies in intensity. Groups with such attitudes and interests may indeed press demands for military expansion on a reluctant government. A final supportive factor, where applicable, is the extent to which armed forces are being maintained for insuring domestic order.

These several factors which have been singled out as political foundations of military power represent a nation's basic mobilizability for purposes of sustaining and using military strength internationally. They preexist the situations in which military questions become acute; they are a mobilization potential. If nations differ in this potential, they tend to react differently to the same kind of external situation that raises the problem of employing military strength.

It should be noted that a nation's entire motivation to support a military buildup or to apply its military power against other states, including the situational factors which are not part of military potential as defined, is a phenomenon of keen interest to statesmen and military leaders. Understanding the entire structure of motivation, which necessarily differs for each situation, is a prerequisite to attempts at predicting a nation's military response to a particular international crisis.

Combinations of Components

Distinguishing these three constituents of military potential—economic and technological, administrative and political—makes it immediately apparent that a given military effort may be based on different combinations of these determinants. Within some range, an inferiority in one can be compensated with superiority in another. A state of superior economic and technological capacity may produce only moderate military forces because its administrative skill is deficient and/or because its propensity to support and to resort to military force is low. A rich nation may prefer not to forego additional consumption in order to maintain large military capabilities. On the other hand, a poor country may produce strong forces, compared with nations of similar size, because it excels in administrative skill and/or because it is willing to pay for military power by reducing consumption. These differences can be of great practical consequence. In 1939–40, for instance, Germany was superior to France in economic and technological capacity, and even more superior in relevant administrative skill and in the political foundations of military power. But though Britain was somewhat inferior to Germany in industrial capacity, she was not inferior to that country in administrative skill and in national propensity to mobilize and use military power. Italy was low on all three kinds of potential.

Foreign Inputs

The various ways in which a government's decision to increase military power or to employ it internationally is affected by its foreign relations are for the most part elements of the external situation to which it is reacting, and have been referred to in Chapter I. Even if it acts primarily in support of a friendly country, whether formally an ally or not, this factor enters into the cost-gain calculations regarding particular military moves in a particular international situation. For example, helping an ally militarily may have pay-offs in terms of a nation's integrity or of long-run security, while failing to honor an alliance commitment may involve costs in terms of international reputation or self-respect. These and similar factors may affect the mobilization of potential, but are not a part of this potential.

However, foreign relations may permit valuable foreign inputs for a state's military sector, which substitute for lacking domestic resources. Thus, by means of international trade, a state may gain access to foreign military technology, *e.g.,* import weapons which it is unable to produce itself, or to produce in sufficient quantity. Similarly, by receiving technical assistance from abroad, a state can obtain valuable administrative skills (*e.g.,* by means of foreign military advisers); and by attracting foreign financial aid, or gifts of military supplies, it can add to indigenous resources. Technological, administrative and economic resources imported from abroad are not, of course, strictly part of a state's military potential. But they add to its military strength, and the ability to obtain such resources from abroad may be regarded as part of a state's potential.

Mobilized Versus Potential Military Strength

The above analysis permits us to understand more clearly differences among states and, over time, for the same state, in the degree to which military potential is transformed into ready force. In the past at any rate, when peace seemed dependable, a nation essentially satisfied with the international *status quo* tended to maintain only small forces in relation to its potential, as did Great Britain and the United States in the early 1930's. When seeking to upset the international *status quo,* if necessary by force, or when confronted with a state displaying an agressive military posture, a nation tended to mobilize more of its potential, as did Germany under Hitler, and the United States in 1940 and 1941 and again in the 1950's. In the past, engagement in major war led to sharp increases in the mobilization of potential, usually far beyond peacetime levels. For example, the military expenditures of the United States rose (in dollars of 1939 purchasing power) from a mere $1.2 billion in 1939 to $13.8 billion in 1941 and $87.5 billion in 1944.[15] In Germany, which had augmented its armaments rapidly before the outbreak of hostilities, government expenditures (mostly for military purposes) expanded (in terms of Marks in 1939 purchasing power) from DM 45 billion in 1939 to DM 70 billion in 1941 and DM 97 billion in 1944.[16] These considerations still apply at the present time, even though deterrence between nuclear powers requires large military outlays at all times.

How much ready military strength a nation develops depends, first and usually foremost, on the expectations of its government and

---

[15]Taken from table in Knorr, *The War Potential of Nations,* p. 233.
[16]*Ibid.,* p. 234.

influential publics about how their interests will be best served in dealing with other states and, second, on domestic uses to which military forces and expenditures can be put. Expectations concerning the outside world, result from a cost-gain calculation, from a balancing of expected advantages and disadvantages foreseen from the maintenance and use of military power at different conceivable levels. Security against foreign aggression, and benefits anticipated from the agressive use of force, have been typical goals which military power was expected to serve. The higher such goals are ranked in relation to other goals and preferences, the larger will be the degree of preferred military mobilization.

However any resulting preference for strong military forces in peacetime, and also in time of war, is checked by an unwillingness to bear the costs. These costs consist necessarily of the frustration of other goals which must be deemphasized or suspended in order to permit the development of military strength. Among the values which must, or may have to be sacrificed, wholly or in part, are consumption and investment for non-military purposes; the personal freedom of youths conscripted for military service; the blunting or infringement of contrary moral sensitivities; the creation of domestic political division; and—as discussed in Chapter I—many other sacrifices of habits antithetical to the military life; and risks involved in the international application of force. And as pointed out in the foregoing analysis, the balancing of advantages and disadvantages, though it takes place in response to the complexion of the international environment, may be conditioned by relatively deep-seated attitudes, developed in the course of historical experience, which, on the part of the nation as a whole, favor or disfavor resort to military power and which, on the part of much of the public, favor or disfavor support of government policy in matters of state involving the use of military power. The direction and strength of these predispositions affect the level of ready military strength which a state will maintain at any one time. One is the utility of armed forces for maintaining domestic order.

Military Potential for Different Types of Conflict

Different uses of military power make demands for different kinds of military forces and, hence indirectly, make different demands on the military potential of states. Deploying a nuclear capability for deterrence, preparing for conventional war, near the state's boundaries or in distant places, possessing capabilities for fighting guerrillas in foreign countries, require different amounts and combinations of economic and technological resources, administrative skills, and also put different burdens on a nation's political foundations of military power. Thus, no states possess now, and only few are able to develop, the scale and kinds of scientific, technological and industrial resources for producing a capacity for nuclear deterrence similar in scale and sophistication to those of the United States and the Soviet Union. The degree of technological and industrial development of states strongly affects the kinds of equipment they can provide for conventional conflict, although imports can to some extent substitute for deficiency in indigenous resources. Conventional forces are ill adapted in terms of weapons, other equipment and training for combatting guerrillas. The need to make a nuclear deterrent threat credible calls for special administrative skills. Employing conventional forces for coercive threats calls for skills different from those involved in the sheer forcible seizure or defense of objects of international contention. Military intervention in foreign civil wars demands different administrative skills, if only because of the high political content of such conflicts, than does the conventional defense of the homeland. Different uses of military power engage the national propensity to mobilize and use military power in different ways. This predisposition may be high for defensive, but low for offensive war, and lower for distant or short wars than for wars close by or for protracted conflict. It may favor the deployment and use of large conventional forces but impede the development and deployment of nuclear arms. The difference in these demands explains why the United States, the world's most powerful country, was in 1967 and 1968 able to deter any nuclear attack, had the capability to wage sizable conventional wars far from its shores, and yet found itself ill-prepared to cope with relatively small numbers of modestly equipped Vietcong in South Vietnam. They also explain why some states did not decide, in the middle 1960's, to develop nuclear weapons even though they were credited with the technological ability to do so.

However, the impact of such different demands of different conflict situations on the properties of ready forces and of military potential is softened by two conditions. First, regarding many military purposes, there is some degree of substitutability of resources. The various elements of combat power can be combined in different ways. Perhaps the most dramatic example of this is provided by the many instances of small bands of guerrillas proving a match for much larger and more heavily equipped conventional troops. The guerrillas were able to compensate for their lack of numbers and equipment by advantages in morale, tactics, information, mobility, and concealment. These are advantages which do not flow from economic and technological capacity, but rather rest on skill and a high propensity for mobilization among the guerrillas and in the local population. On the other hand, a large and industrially resourceful state fighting local insurgents in foreign territories may precisely substitute superior numbers and sophisticated special equipment (for example, helicopters) in order to offset the advantages possessed by guerrillas. Similarly, in conventional war on or close to its own territory, a belligerent state which is inferior in technological and industrial resources may compensate for this weakness by means of larger forces able to move without mobilized transport, to endure field conditions with a minimum of comfort, and perhaps inspired by superior discipline. These sorts of factors accounted for the relative success of the Chinese armies fighting American forces in Korea.

In addition to the possibilities of substitution, it may also be noted that, though ready military forces are limited in their versatility, military potential is naturally more adaptable. The extent of this adaptability depends on the richness of the resource base. A state with abundant industrial, technological, and administrative resources is able not only to afford more versatility in its ready forces than less well endowed states do; it is also able, in the event of need, to produce new kinds of military capabilities, and their resource structure may be resilient enough to do so without much delay.

But the possibilities of substitution are always limited at any one time. Superior number or morale may be no match for an opponent greatly superior in military technology; superiority in conventional forces is of little avail against a foe possessing nuclear armament, etc. The adaptability of military potential is similarly limited except over long periods of time. The conclusion remains that the military potential of states is not equally adapted to the production of different forces, and to all possible uses of force.

Measurement

We have concluded above that it is difficult, if not impossible, to measure and compare the combat power of different national military forces even if we disregard the complication arising from different kinds of military conflict and theaters of war. It is equally difficult to measure and compare the military potential of states. Even the measurement and comparison of economic capacity in aggregates is beset by conceptual and statistical difficulties. And how do we measure administrative skill or the political foundations of military power? The broad constituents of military potential contain many diverse elements, most of which resist measurement, and which are apt to be variously combined in different states. Even if we could measure all these elements, how could we measure and compare the broader aggregates, or military potential as a whole, as long as our units of measurement are incommensurable?

Despite these predicaments, there are modest possibilities of assessment and comparison. If this were not so, statesmen and the intelligence services of states would abandon all attempts at estimating military potential. Few fragments of potential are measurable in any rigorous sense; the evaluation of non-quantitative factors will depend on judgment as well as information which is often vague, ambiguous and obsolete; and the resulting assessments and comparisons cannot claim to be other than rough. But once an analytical structure has been developed for the study of military potential, it is possible to identify the information one should like to have and to search for reasonably good indicators which express, even if only grossly, the magnitude of various elements of potential. An abundance of indicators is in fact on hand for appraising economic capacity, and even technological capacity has been measured to a degree. No such good indicators are readily available for assessing administrative skill and the political foundation of military power. With these factors little more can be done than classifying states in such very crude terms as "high" and "low," and even such modest appraisals, it must be assumed, may rest on faulty judgment. There is always the hope that further progress in the social sciences will gradually permit more complete and more accurate assessments and comparisons of national military potential. In this respect, the student of military potential is not worse off than the student of political development, and of many other aspects of national life.

Geographic Aspects

Since all elements of military power have a specific location on the earth, and are affected by the peculiarities of their location, there is none which does not have geographic aspects. However, most of what would concern a geographer interested in military potential can be and is included under non-geographic concepts. Climate and national resources concern the economist because they affect national production; topographical or other physical barriers within states may interest the political scientist because they affect political integration, etc. But three geographic phenomena merit brief discussion because they are often singled out for their peculiar bearing on military power and are neglected in the following analysis.

Climate

Aside from the obvious fact that climate affects agriculture production, the geographic location of great military powers in recent centuries has caused people to muse whether location in the temperate zone, rather than in the subtropical or tropical zones, is not a controlling condition of power, and hence a vital constituent of military potential.[17]

A look at the current map of industrial and military power—with the United States, Soviet Union, Britain, France, West Germany and Japan all located in northern latitudes—seems to suggest that this question turns on plausible implications. (The southern hemisphere has a much smaller land mass than the northern one, and a still smaller proportion of land with a climate resembling that of the

[17]For a sensible discussion see A.F.K. Organski, *World Politics*, Sec. Ed., New York, Knopf, 1968, pp. 130–133. Also Louis C. Peltier and G. Etzel Pearcy, *Military Geography*, Princeton, Van Nostrand, 1966.

moderately northern latitudes.) There is, however, so far no scientific confirmation of the theory. The military dominance of northern states in recent centuries resulted from the birth and evolution of the scientific and technological evolution in western Europe. This unique revolution originated there for reasons which, though remaining unclear, are not usually attached to climate, and spread initially through Europe and to the areas settled by Europeans overseas. But one must not forget that the industrial revolution was favored, in the early phases, by the presence of coal and iron deposits which were discovered first, in large and easily exploitable quantities, in the northern lands. Although this is, of course, a geographic factor, it is not one of climate. One must not forget either that, through the ancient and Middle Ages, northern peoples were not, as a general rule, militarily superior to southern populations. In ancient times, the Egyptian, Carthaginian and Mohammedan empires were certainly imposing military agglomerates, and Rome, which dominated the dense and dank forests of the north for so long, was not exactly based on lands and peoples living under a decidedly northern climate. It cannot be denied that climate may have an indirect influence on the geographic distribution of the kinds of human productivity in which military power is rooted. But even if this possibility is granted, the question arises of whether, in modern times, science and technology will not tend to reduce any differences resulting from the incidence of climate, and therefore whether this factor of climate is now of as much consequence as it may have been earlier.

Size of National Land Area

Size of geographic space *per se* is of little, if any, importance as a basis of national military power. There certainly is no strong correlation between national military power and the size of national territory. Of course, the Soviet Union ranks first in size and territory, and the United States fourth. But Canada ranks second, Brazil fifth, Australia sixth, Argentina eighth, and the Sudan ninth. It is also evident that states with tiny territories have rarely figured as great military powers. The fact is that space gains its significance from what is in it—people and resources; and what little correlation there is between size of territory and military power results from the obvious fact that, on the basis of statistical probability, the more area a state occupies, the more content, which is significant for power it tends to have. It is also true, historically, that military powers tended to expand territory either by an outward pushing of state boundaries into contiguous territory, or by the acquistion of colonial territories. But this represents an effect on, not of, geography.

Large areas with no or scant population and resources tend to be an economic burden, especially costly in terms of transportation, and also an impediment to military deployment. Since they must be protected, they tend to be deficit areas as far as military potential is concerned. However, they also obstruct foreign aggressors. For this reason, in the past, historically viewed, large space has also been of considerable defensive value to states. A state of vast expanse could lose a great deal of territory to invading armies without endangering the center of military power. Space could be traded for time required for converting more military potential into combat force, or space could be given up in order to drain the opponent's resources in an increasing logistical effort. As the French and German invasions of Russia, and the Japanese invasion of China (1933–45), demonstrated, or earlier British resistance to American independence, the conquest and control of huge populated areas presented the conquering power with a formidable, and sometimes prohibitive logistical task. As we shall see in the following section, modern technology tends to diminish this refractory quality of space. There is, however, one consideration which makes sheer size of territory an asset in strategic nuclear warfare. Large territorial space may have led to a lesser geographic concentration of population and industry than is characteristic of small industrial countries, and large states present thus a larger number of independent targets for nuclear deterrence. However, as Australia and Canada make amply clear, the mere availability of space does not necessarily engender this consequence. Nevertheless, Japan and England are far more densely settled targets than the United States or the Soviet Union. In any case, vast expanse of terriotry *perm* ᵗᶜ decentralization of population and industry with reference to the threat of nuclear war, and also favors the dispersed location of nuclear retaliatory forces away from population centers.

Location and Distance

Geographic location on the earth has influenced foreign policy, military strategy and military capability in many ways throughout history. It affects military accessibility and vulnerability as well as military mobility. For example, the fact that Russia has lacked adequate warm-water ports (exit from the Black Sea being controlled by the power occupying the Dardanelles), has always made it and still makes it, difficult for it to develop sea power and hence the effective military reach which maritime strength can supply. Britain, the United States and Japan have been greatly favored in this respect. As the extreme examples of Belgium (or Poland) and New Zealand (or Chile) show, location on the crossroads of larger military powers has spelled military vulnerability and insecurity, while geographic isolation has been a distinct asset from this point of view.

The weightiest effect of location on the exertion of military strength has been distance, that is, the cost of transferring military force across space. The transmission of combat force over long distances is very costly of economic resources which otherwise could be used to produce more military forces.[18] This "loss-of-strength gradient,"[19] applying over the tremendous distance of theater of war from the bases of Russian military power, is the major reason why, in 1905, Russia, then a nation of 142 million, was defeated by Japan, then a country with 45 million. At the beginning of World War II in 1939, the American merchant marine totaled about 1,150 ocean-going vessels and 10.5 million deadweight tons. By the time Germany surrendered in 1945, the United States had built another 5,200 ships totaling almost 53.0 million tons.[20] If the steel, manpower and other resources which went into constructing the shipyards and into building, manning and fueling these ships could have been saved, the United States could have greatly and more swiftly expanded its armed forces.

This resource cost of lengthy supply chains is not, of course, measured by sheer distance. It varies with other geographic conditions (notably topography and access by water), with the supply-dependence of troops and with transport technology. Mountains, deserts, swamps and forests increase the cost and difficulty of transportation over land. Military forces differ greatly in their ability "to live on the land," in the amount of gear, foods and comforts they require; motorized troops need vehicles, spare parts, gasoline and oil; military aircraft need airfields, spare parts and fuel; etc. During the Korean War, for example, the supply dependence of the average American soldier was a large multiple, in terms of tonnage, of that of the average Chinese soldier. Transportation technology has a central bearing on costs. Water transport has always been cheaper per mile than transportation on land. With modern marine technology especially, the cost of loading and unloading, which are also being cut sharply by innovation, constitute a large proportion of total shipping costs, so that the addition of miles of transit, which is variable, contributes less than proportionally to the overall logistical burden. Sheer distance, therefore, bears no simple relation to military strength.[21] Recent advances in air transport also cut the adverse effect of distance for military units or weapons which weigh little, or occupy small space, in relation to military value.

In addition to progress in transport technology, advances in military technology itself have greatly qualified space and distance as a barrier to the geographic reach of military force. This holds true particularly of intercontinental aircraft and missiles which, when equipped with nuclear explosives, pack awesome destructive power in each unit. However, as indicated by the American effort in

---

[18]*Cf.* Knorr, *The War Potential of Nations*, pp. 52–54.
[19]*Cf.* Kenneth E. Boulding, *Conflict and Defense* (New York: Harper & Row, 1962), pp. 245–247.
[20]Donald M. Nelson, *Arsenal of Democracy* (New York: Harcourt, Brace & World, 1946), p. 243.
[21]On these matters, see Albert Wohlstetter, "Illusions of Distance," *Foreign Affairs*, v. 46, January 1968, pp. 242–255.

Vietnam, which by 1967 involved a tremendous logistical investment, distance remains a costly impediment in non-nuclear and local war. To be sure, the speed with which military forces can move over land and by sea has strikingly increased since the wars of the Napoleonic era, or even since World Wars I and II. But the quantity of military materiel to be moved has also expanded, perhaps to a similar extent (excepting nuclear technology). Just because the geographic transfer of military force remains costly, the industrial states with a large economic potential have an advantage in coping with it.

3 Economic Capacity

Whenever a nation maintains armed forces, carries on military research and development, or undertakes other military tasks, it assigns a proportion of its manpower and other productive resources to the military sector of its activities. A part of its manpower and resources from which the military sector is fed, constitute the nation's military economic potential. Whenever a nation expands its military effort by allocating more manpower and resources to the military sector, it is mobilizing an additional proportion of its potential.

Since societies must at all times feed, clothe and house their members, and carry on various non-military activities, only a fraction of total manpower and resources is ever available for the military sector. Even in extreme emergencies, this fraction will rarely exceed half of productive capacity. At the height of World War II, the war absorbed 55 percent of Britain's Gross National Product in 1943, and 50 percent of Germany's in 1944.[1] Furthermore, the claims of the military sector fall unevenly on the nation's economic capacity. It will fall more heavily on men of military age than on males of other age groups; and it will fall more heavily on armament and defense-related industries than on others. As we will see below, there is no definite limit at which civilian consumption, non-military investment, and public services are irreducible. There is no empirical or theoretical basis for fixing the proportion of manpower and resources—in the aggregate or in their divisions—which can be regarded definitely as a nation's economic military potential. In time of peace or war, this line

[1]Knorr, *The War Potential of Nations*, pp. 238–239.

is variable, fixed only with reference to specific situations; and in each particular situation the line will be determined by many factors. Since all nations are subject to limitations, however, on the extent to which resources can and will be spared for the military sector, their overall capacity is nevertheless an important indicator of economic military potential.

Like the study of military power and military capabilities, the study of economic military potential is inevitably comparative. States obviously differ greatly in their economic capacity and hence in their potential. However, in evaluating these differences in economic capacity, several considerations must always be kept in mind. First, the importance of national economic capacity is proportionate to the demands on manpower and other economic resources made by different kinds of national military effort. This importance will be great in a prolonged and intensive arms race or in large-scale and protracted military conflict. But it will be small in the management of border skirmishes or in putting troops on alert when a military threat is made or countered. Second, the larger the national economic capacity of a state, the less it will be absorbed by a military effort of a given size in terms of resource demands. The fact that the United States could fight a sizeable war in South Vietnam in 1967 at a budget outlay then amounting to little more than 3 percent of the GNP— which clearly did not tax its *economic* capacity very much—simply reflects on the country's huge economic military potential. The same kind of war would have strained the resources of a smaller power with a potential similar to that of France or the United Kingdom. Third, moderate differences in the manpower and economic capacity of states are inconsequential for the study of economic military potential, partly because economic information is not accurate and comparable enough, but chiefly because such differences are easily offset by differences in the other bases of military strength. The less unequal opponents are in economic capacity, the greater the tendency for differences in military performance to result from differences in the will to prevail militarily and the skill with which mobilization is managed. Fourth, it is therefore different orders of magnitude in manpower and economic capacity, and in related characteristics, that are of primary interest in studying economic military potential. Fifth, to reemphasize, economic capacity is merely potential. Its mobilization requires the will to allocate resources to the military sector. Potential is permissive. It does not insure mobilization.

The allocation of resources to the military sector is reflected in government military expenditures. As indicated in Chapter II, there are several factors which determine the level of military expenditures undertaken by states. For example, one would expect foreign entanglements, which pose military risks, to be a weighty factor. The arms outlays of states in the Near East, where such entanglement is intense, have been larger in terms of GNP than for most Latin American countries which have been spared such involvements for a long period of time. Thus in 1965, expressed as a percentage of GNP, military expenditures were only 2.9 for Brazil, 2.0 for Chile, 1.7 for Argentina, and .8 for Mexico (but 7.1 percent for Cuba!), while they were 13.0 for Jordan, 12.2 for Israel, 8.4 for Syria, and 8.3 for the U.A.R. For countries at war, the proportion would be bigger. In 1965, it was 19.7 for the Republic of North Vietnam.[2]

However, Table 1 reveals a remarkably strong correlation between the national military expenditures and GNP. Of the ten countries ranking first to tenth in military outlays all but one rank among the first ten in GNP. The exception—Japan—is explained by the fact that constitutional provisions severely limit its military forces. Of the countries ranking eleventh to twentieth in military expenditures all but two are among those ranking eleventh to twentieth in GNP. The six countries with the largest GNP (the United States, the Soviet Union, Japan, West Germany, Britain, and France) accounted for 77.0 percent of world military expenditures in 1965.

GNP reflects both the size of countries, in terms of population, and their stage of economic development, as expressed in GNP per capita. Some countries of medium population have large GNPs because they are highly developed economically; other countries, at a relatively low level of development, have large GNPs because they have very numerous populations. The six countries with the largest populations (China, India, the Soviet Union, the United States, Pakistan and Indonesia) contributed 70.6 percent to world military outlays. But in both groups of six countries, the large military efforts of the United States and the Soviet Union dominate the picture, accounting for nearly two thirds of world military expenditures. If we exclude these two states, we find that the other four states with large GNP's accounted for 12.8 percent, and the other four countries with the largest population for 6.6 percent of world military outlays. The twenty countries with the largest per-capita GNP's accounted for 85.7 percent. All countries in this group are European or North American with the exception of Japan, Australia, and New Zealand. It is worth noting that all 99 countries, including such large ones as China, India, Pakistan, Indonesia, and Brazil, accounted for the remaining 14.3 percent.

On the basis of military expenditures, the United States and the Soviet Union are clearly in a class by themselves. The Soviet Union, which spends less than the United States, still spent nearly seven times the amount spent by France in 1965. These are the great military powers, or the so-called superpowers. There is a second group of major military powers, or middle powers, with military expenditures at least twice that of any of the remaining countries. These middle powers are Mainland China, France, the United Kingdom and West

---

[2]Data obtained from U.S. Arms Control and Disarmament Agency, *World-Wide Military Expenditures and Related Data, Calendar Year 1965,* Research Report 67–6 (Washington , D.C., 1967).

TABLE 1
Ranking of Major Countries According to Military
Expenditures and Gross National Product, 1965[3]
(expressed in purchasing power equivalents, current dollars)

Country	Military Expenditures		GNP		Per Capita GNP	
	Rank	Total (mil. $)	Rank	Total (bil. $)	Rank	Total
United States	1	51,840	1	683.9	1	$3,510
Soviet Union	2	40,000[a]	2	313.0[a]	12	1,360
France	3	6,100	6	105.8	5	1,910
Mainland China	4	6,000[e]	7	76.0	23	100
United Kingdom	5	5,621	5	112.0	7	1,820
West Germany	6	4,991	4	124.7	6	1,900
Italy	7	2,509	8	69.8	13	1,100
Canada	8	1,724	9	53.7	3	2,450
India	9	1,710	10	40.5	23	100
Poland	10	1,700[e]	11	30.8	14	980
Japan	11	1,622	3	175.0	15	860
Czechoslovakia	12	1,300[2]	18	22.1	10	1,560
Sweden	13	1,230	14	28.1	2	2,500
Australia	14	1,080	15	27.9	4	1,980
Indonesia	15	1,000[e]	29	10.4	23	100
East Germany	16	1,000[e]	16	26.6	9	1,570
Netherlands	17	980	17	23.0	11	1,540
Brazil	18	961	13	28.4	20	270
Belgium	19	816	19	20.9	8	1,760
Spain	20	785	12	29.6	17	690
Yugoslavia	21	624	25	14.4	19	450
UAR	22	532	36	6.4	22	160
South Africa	23	510	22	16.9	18	530
Rumania	24	500[e]	24	14.8	16	780
Turkey	25	500	31	9.6	21	260
Pakistan	26	494	32	9.3	23	100

[a]A representative ratio of military expenditures to GNP cannot be derived from the
dollar estimates given for the Soviet Union because the conversion rate used to express
Soviet GNP in dollar equivalents differs from that for Soviet military expenditures.
[e]Estimate

Germany. A third group of 18 countries allocated at least $500 million
to military purposes in 1965: Canada, Brazil, Italy, Spain, Netherlands, Belgium, Sweden, East Germany, Poland, Czechoslovakia, Hungary, Rumania, Bulgaria, Turkey, India, Indonesia, Japan, and Australia. It is striking that of all 24 states mentioned, all but five are
European countries or countries of European settlement overseas.

The ten largest spenders on military affairs spent between 3 and 10
percent of their GNP. Of 120 countries, 81 states spent between 2 and
10 percent. The variation in these patterns of military expenditures is
obviously far smaller than in the size of national GNP's. Indisputably,

[3]Adapted from *ibid.*

government decisions on military budgets do not follow directly from the size of the GNP, and from changes thereof, but turn on essentially political and military considerations. Yet whatever the configuration of government motives which causes this pattern, the fact is that the more economic resources, and hence the more economic military potential, countries have, the more they tend to expend on their military establishments. The correlation between military outlays and GNP's being very close, it is appropriate to begin the study of economic military potential with a consideration of the GNP of states.

Gross National Product

At any one time, the economic resources available to a nation— whether for purposes of satisfying consumption, investment or defense—are (a) its labor force, *i.e*, workers of all kinds and skills, including scientists, teachers, businessmen, bureaucrats and politicians; (b) its stock of real capital, in the form of plant, durable producers' equipment, and inventories of raw materials, semi-finished goods, and finished goods not yet sold to consumers; (c) its land, including vegetation, water and mineral deposits; and (d) its net monetary claims on foreigners, for these claims can be exchanged for unrequited imports of goods and services, which involves a draft on foreign resources. These productive factors, together with goods in consumers' hands, comprise the wealth of nations. Stocks of money are no part of it. In allocating productive resources to the military sector of society, the management of money is an administrative problem. But money constitutes only a claim on goods and services, and on productive factors. With the exception of claims on foreigners noted above, it is not itself a productive resource.

However, since nations vary greatly in the composition and quality, as well as the magnitude, of their productive resources, direct comparisons can be made only of selected and fairly homogeneous components. The only possibility for *overall* comparison is indirect and is accomplished by comparing the output which these resources produce during a specific period of time. This measure is the Gross National Product. It equals the value, at prices set by the market or government authorities, of all final goods and services produced by the national economy during a year. Since figures for the GNP and its divisions are reported for all countries in terms of their monetary unit, and since these values are convertible into one currency, it is possible to compare the overall economic capacity of states.

The GNP is far from an ideal measure of the overall economic capability of nations, and inter-economy comparisons are beset with pitfalls and incapable of exactitude.[4] GNP figures are estimates

[4]Readers interested in a detailed discussion of these difficulties are referred to the relevant economics literature. Any good introductory textbook will analyze the essential points and contain references to specialist treatments.

including a varying element of guesswork. The GNP reflects only productive resources actually employed during the period. Some government expenditures, although commonly included in the GNP, are actually intermediate services which should be regarded as costs of production (*e.g.*, the output of regulatory agencies). Some consumption items (*e.g.*, private expenditures on education) could be regarded as investment, that is, investment in human resources which are omitted from investment figures. International comparisons of GNP have only limited validity for several additional reasons. All governments do not use the same definitions and measurement practices. The range of production covered in GNP figures varies. This difference is especially great among countries at different stages of economic development. Thus, in economically less developed countries, a great many services are performed within consumption units (for example, laundering and bread-baking), without entering commercial transactions, and are excluded from the GNP, while such service products are included in the GNP as, with increasing economic development, they become commercialized.

But the worst impediment to comparison is that GNP's are expressed in different currencies and reflect a different composition of goods and services exchanged at different prices. Converting GNP's into the same national currency at official exchange rates is apt to yield more or less misleading results because official exchange rates may unrealistically exaggerate the purchasing power of one currency as against another. Conversion would avoid error only if all goods and services in both countries sold at the same price ratios, and if the exchange rate faithfully reflected the purchasing power of each monetary unit. But such conditions do not prevail in the real world. A way to deal with this problem is to compute the value of production in both countries by applying the prices of one. This procedure of using "purchasing power equivalents" was employed in constructing the data from which Table 1 was adapted. But if this method is followed, two different weights can be chosen; and it makes a great deal of difference which country's prices are used. For example, a pioneering study on this subject showed the GNP of Great Britain in 1955 to have been either 16 or 20 percent of the GNP of the United States, depending on whether European or American price ratios were applied.[5] There is no logical preference for either result, or for settling on the average amount.

These shortcomings of GNP comparisons make it clear that these value aggregates are only a very rough index of national productive capacity, and that international comparisons are inevitably crude, lending significance to only large differences. Yet they are the only basis for comparing the overall resources of nation states; and, if taken

[5]Milton Gilbert and associates, *Comparative National Products and Price Levels* (Paris: Organization for European Economic Cooperation, n.d.), p. 86.

with proper caution, they permit us to get an approximate picture of reality.

The same problems are encountered when national military budgets are compared. Thus, some states include items in this budget which other states include in other parts of government expenditures. Taking account of differences in relative prices again constitutes a difficult obstacle. In some countries, the prices of goods and services entering the military sector are markedly higher in relation to the general price level than is the case in other countries. In the study already mentioned, the defense expenditures of the United Kingdom were $7.1 billion when U.S. price weights were used, but only $5.1 billion when European price weights were applied.[6] According to American experts, absolute Soviet defense outlays and their share in the GNP are appreciably higher than appears from official Soviet statistics.[7]

In a world in which everywhere resources are inevitably scarce in relation to various demands made on them, the overall availability of resources limits the ability of governments to develop, maintain, and employ military strength. Despite several drawbacks to the comparison of GNP's, the GNP is the best guide for comparing the economic capacity of states. It made an appreciable difference in this respect that, in the mid-1960's, the GNP of the United States was more than twice that of the Soviet Union, or that China's was appreciably smaller than that of either France or West Germany, and only a little more than one tenth of that of the United States.

The Uses of GNP

The uses of the GNP are broken down customarily into several expenditure categories: private consumption, gross domestic investment, net exports or imports, and public expenditures. In free-enterprise countries, investments are mostly private business investments, their share varying with the prevailing extent of private as against public enterprise. When military outlays, which are part of public expenditures, rise—as they may in the event of a severe and prolonged international crisis, an arms race, or war—other expenditures are necessarily affected, regardless of the type of economic system. They need not contract in absolute amount, provided the GNP is expanding enough to cover the increase in military expenditures. Nor need all other kinds of expenditures contract. But together they must fall in relation to military outlays, in exactly the proportion by which military expenditures amount.

This is shown in Table 2. As the United States became involved

[6]*Ibid.*
[7]*Cf.* Abraham S. Becker, *Soviet Military Outlays,* RAND Corp. Memorandum RM 3886 (Santa Monica, July 1964).

TABLE 2

Year	Personal Consumption	Gross Private Dom. Investment	Defense Expend.	Other Public Expenditure	GNP	Defense Expenditures
	Percentages of GNP				Billions of dollars	
1939	73.9	10.3	1.3	13.4	90.5	1.2
1944	51.6	3.4	42.4	3.6	210.1	87.4
1947	70.0	14.7	4.0	7.0	231.3	9.1
1951	62.8	18.1	10.2	7.7	328.4	33.6
1951	62.7	15.0	13.3	8.3	345.5	45.9
1960	64.6	14.8	8.9	10.9	503.7	44.9
1966	62.7	15.9	8.1	12.6	743.3	60.5
1967	62.6	14.3	9.2	14.4	785.1	72.6

[a]Table omits net exports of goods and services.

in a large-scale prolonged war of attrition, military expenditures in 1944 were about 33 times what they had been in 1939. Therefore, although the GNP expanded hugely, chiefly because a large volume of productive resources had been unemployed in 1939, the share of personal consumption expenditures and gross investment, and other public expenditures, suffered drastic cutbacks. By 1947 the United States had demobilized the large bulk of its military forces, defense outlays had fallen back to 4 percent of the GNP, and other expenditures had risen to normal levels. The experience of other countries has been similar to that of the United States. During World War II, for example, personal consumption in Germany fell from 81 percent of GNP in 1940 to 59 percent in 1944 when the total product had expanded by 28 percent. Gross domestic private investment decreased from 14 to 3 percent over the same period.[9]

Even when a nation wages a very exacting and prolonged war, personal consumption must obviously remain a major claim on existing resources. Not all non-defense expenditures of government, central and local, can be reduced since education and many other services must continue, even if perhaps on a diminished scale. And some investments must be made if only in order to maintain capital resources, or to produce new ones, required for the expanded production of military supplies. In fact, although a country only forgoes capital-induced economic growth as net investment is decreased, if the maintenance of existing capital is also neglected, it uses up

[8]Adapted from Council of Economic Advisers, *Economic Report of the President* (Washington, D.C., 1968), p. 209.
[9]Knorr, *The War Potential of Nations*, pp. 232 ff. For more details on changes in resource availability and use during World War II, See the same, ch. 12.

productive resources. If prolonged, such capital consumption will cause GNP to diminish.

A large and growing economy can easily absorb the burden of limited war. For instance, much of the increase in American defense expenditures occasioned by the Korean and Vietnamese wars came from an expanding GNP. During both wars, the absolute volume of consumption and non-military public expenditures rose—although less than they would have risen presumably in the absence of war, and consumption declined as a percentage of GNP. In 1952 and 1967, gross private domestic investment also declined as a percentage of GNP from what it had been in the preceeding year. In absolute amounts, it was lower in 1952, 1953 and 1954 than in 1951; and in 1967 it was lower than in 1966.

As these examples suggest, the economic ability to sustain national military efforts is primarily a function both in the size and growth of GNP and of the degree to which other than military uses of the GNP can be *compressed.* However, in addition to the prevailing rate of economic growth and the compressibility of consumption, investment and non-military public expenditures, there are three special sources of *expansion* which may provide economic support for a military effort. One concerns international economic transactions, which will be discussed subsequently. The second is the employment of productive resources which had failed to find employment before the military effort got underway. Thus, the United States and other countries were able to support a large part of their efforts during World War II by utilizing workers, plant, equipment and land that had been kept idle by the severe worldwide economic slump of the 1930's. In the United States, the number of unemployed workers fell from 9.5 million in 1939 to 670,000 in 1944; and in Britain they fell from 1.7 million in 1938 to 54,000 in 1944.[10] This opportunity to increase production is not, of course, available in free-enterprise economies which are already operating at full employment when an extra demand on resources is made. Nor is it available in socialist economies where, though structural unemployment or underemployment may appear, this kind of cyclical depression does not occur. The third source of expansion is that the supply of labor may grow either as a result of natural population increase or because, in an emergency, people who do not normally seek employment can be induced to join the labor force, and the hours of work can be increased.

The "Disposable Surplus"

The sources from which productive resources can be drawn for the military sector may be summarized as follows:

[10] *Ibid.,* pp. 242–243.

	(1) Gross National Product prior to Increase in Military Demand
plus	(2) Output of Productive Reserves or Natural Additions to Labor Force
minus	(3) Reduced Civilian Consumption
minus	(4) Reduced Gross Private Domestic Investment
minus	(5) Reduced Non-Military Purchases of Government
minus/plus	(6) Change in Net Foreign Investment
minus/plus	(7) Change in Labor Productivity
equals	(8) Disposable Surplus for military Sector

The difference between (1) + (2) − (3) to (7) has sometimes been called the "disposable surplus for war," comprising the true military economic potential of states. However, though this concept lends itself to a statistical representation of what happens when a nation shifts economic resources to producing military strength, the surplus in question is not only a variable which defies precise prediction; it also is not a residue which results automatically after someone, presumably the government, has fixed, first, the overall complex of resources and, then, the curtailment of non-military expenditures. Governments do have varying degrees of influence on the supply and employment of resources—an influence derived from their political capacity—but this influence falls far short of control.

To conclude, a large GNP *permits* a large military effort as far as economic capacity is concerned. It does not determine the magnitude of the effort. We note that Japan in the 1960's had a big and very productive economy but maintained only strikingly modest security forces. The crucial question is how much of this economic capacity will be allocated to military purposes in the event of need, and this is a problem of political potential. Everything else being the same, a state allocating 20 percent of its GNP to the military sector can be a match for a country with a GNP twice as large but allotting only 10 percent to military purposes. Such differences in allocation, rather than in GNP, may be especially important in limited military conflicts or in moderate arms races, in contrast to large-scale and long wars of attrition.[11]

In the event of limited conflicts, it is the appropriate military forces in existence which tend to be important or even decisive in the outcome, when there is neither time nor incentive to proceed to the level of mobilization on which sheer productive capacity would make its weight felt. Similarly, this factor is apt to be less important in a limited arms race between two or more powers. Nevertheless, a large GNP represents an ability to make a large military effort. This ability is what potential means.

[11]James R. Schlesinger, *The Political Economy of National Security* (New York: Frederick A. Praeger, 1960), p. 72.

Gross National Product Per Capita

Size of GNP depends on magnitude and productivity of a nation's labor force. High productivity is reflected in a large GNP per head of the population. As Table 3 indicates, nations which differ in their stage of economic development, differ markedly in GNP per capita.

Except for affecting the absolute size of GNP's, differences in GNP per capita have no direct and simple bearing on differences in national military power. There certainly is very little relationship between military expenditures and GNP per capita as such. Iceland has one of the highest per-capita incomes in the world, but maintains no military establishment whatever, whereas China, with a GNP per capita only one twenty-fifth of Iceland's, has 2.5 million men under arms. However, since a high GNP per capita usually indicates an advanced level of economic and technological development, it is to that extent also an index of the ability to produce and use complicated military materiel. Even this ability acquires significance as military economic potential only when related to size of population and economy, and of course to the actual or potential military strength of other states. To command a GNP per capita of $1,750, as Finland did in 1965, did not give her much of an economic military potential *vis-à-vis* the Soviet Union, whose GNP per capita was $1,358. Nor could Kuwait, with 475,000 people, whose enormous oil production gave her an astounding GNP of $3,196 per capita, hope to generate much military power *vis-a-vis* Iran with 24 million inhabitants and a GNP of only $241 per capita. In studying military economic potential,

TABLE 3
Gross National Product Per Capita, 1965[12]
Selected Countries
(Dollars)

Above $1,500		$1,499-$500		$499-$200		Below $200	
United States	3,514	Czechoslovakia	1,556[a]	Chile	485	Nigeria	114
Sweden	2,499	Soviet Union	1,358[b]	Cuba	411	S. Korea	102
Canada	2,450	Israel	1,325	Malaysia	296	China	101
Australia	1,980	Japan	863	Brazil	270	India	100
France	1,907	Rumania	779[a]	Turkey	261	Indonesia	100
West Germany	1,902	Argentina	722	Iran	241	Pakistan	97
Britain	1,816	Spain	688	Algeria	225	Kenya	90

[a]Expressed in rough purchasing power equivalents.
[b]Different conversion rates, in purchasing power terms, used for different items.

[12]Adapted from U.S. Arms Control and Disarmament Agency, *World-Wide Military Expenditures and Related Data*, pp. 8–12.

the item of GNP per capita must be evaluated in association with other relevant data.

The development of nuclear bombs by Mainland China in the 1960's furnishes a telling example. In 1965, the Chinese GNP was perhaps little more than one-twentieth of the French. Indeed, the entire GNP of China, with 755 million people, was somewhat smaller than that of France with a population of only 49 million. On the whole, the Chinese economy was and is vastly underdeveloped compared with the French. Yet China beat France in the development of nuclear explosives[13] which are among the technologically most sophisticated of modern weapons. Since the Chinese nuclear program is shrouded in secrecy, and since we are far less familiar with Chinese polity and economy than with France, we do not have the evidence to explain the Chinese success. However, it is known that Mainland China possessed scientific, technological, and industrial resources which, though small in relation to population, were in absolute volume much closer to French resources than the ratio of per-capita figures suggests. Since an effort to develop nuclear bombs does not demand a massive application of resources, we may surmise that China's success is attributed to the following factors. First, Mainland China possessed scientists, engineers and other required resources of adequate quality and in sufficient quantity. In this respect, it should be noted that Mainland China is unlike many other countries of low per-capita income in that it has behind it more than a millenium of high civilization, emphasizing scholarship; that many Chinese scientists received excellent training in the United States and other technologically advanced countries; and that a number of manufacturing industries had been established under foreign management or with foreign assistance. These are matters of economic and technological potential. Second, the Chinese government was willing and able to allocate the necessary resources, which were no doubt needed also for other purposes, to the nuclear program. This is a factor of political will and authority. Third, the Chinese program may have enjoyed better direction than the French, which is a question of administrative skill.

However, the fact remains that, among states of comparable size, substantial differences in economic and industrial development, as reflected in gross differences in GNP per capita, determined the kinds of military equipment and forces which they can produce from indigenous resources.

The question has been raised whether it is not easier for a wealthy nation to compress private consumption than for a poor country where most people live close to subsistence level; and whether populations in countries with high incomes per capita are not in possession of large inventories of consumers' goods (*e.g.,*

---

[13]*Cf.* B.W. Augenstein, "The Chinese and French Programs for the Development of National Nuclear Forces," *Orbis,* XI (Fall 1967), pp. 846–848.

automobiles, household appliances, clothing) which permit them to carry on for a long time before lack of replacements enforces cuts in consumption patterns. Thus the productive factors turning out a large proportion of consumption goods in rich societies, and perhaps all consumption goods above the level of subsistence, might be thought to constitute a reserve capacity which in an emergency could be assigned to the military sector; and that such reallocation of resources is facilitated by the presence of accumulated "fat" in the form of a durable and semi-durable consumers goods. It is implicit in this notion that wealthy societies have a larger "disposable surplus" for military purposes than poor ones do, and that, as far as consumption goes, absolute subsistence needs fix the lower limit to this surplus, the crest of previous consumption setting the upper limit.

This is, however, a dubious notion. To begin with, the concept of "subsistence level" is extremely ambiguous. Although undernourishment, malnutrition, inadequate shelter, lack of medical care, etc. are known to affect the productivity of labor, it has proved difficult to estimate "minimum requirements of subsistence" as determined by physiological needs; in any case, these would vary with climate, work, the average weight of individuals in different populations, and similar factors.[14] Furthermore, it is naive to assume that subsistence is solely or even mainly derived from physiological needs. It clearly varies with the stage of economic development, the degree of urbanization, cultural conditions, etc. Even the "necessities of life"—in terms of housing, clothing, transportation, and other forms of consumption—ascend with economic development and rising incomes. In fact, consumer "needs" are highly sensitive to habits and attitudes.[15] Many items of consumption, though not necessary to sustaining life, are tied to strong habits, and hence they are not discretionary, that is, postponable. If minimum consumption requirements are largely determined by what a society, and its several parts, are accustomed to enjoy and expect, then they are utterly different for the inhabitants of Paris and Papua. However much physiological needs may vary, subsistence needs as fixed by habit and expectation vary a great deal more. The Parisian cannot be expected to function, if reduced to the Papuan's level of consumption, precisely because consumption above the level of physiological need is largely not a luxury. If measured in terms of frustrated wants, the consumption sacrifices of different populations could be equal at vastly diverging levels of consumption. We may infer that there are great differences in the consumption levels below which the productivity of various members of national labor forces, including the military, is no longer sustained. How much consumption *above* these levels can be lowered depends on the sacrifices which a population is willing, or

[14]*Cf.* M.K. Bennett, *The World's Food* (New York: Harper and Row, 1954), part III.
[15]George Katona, *The Powerful Consumer* (New York: McGraw-Hill, 1960), esp. chs. 4–6, 8–10.

can be made, to accept. This compressibility varies both in high- and in low-income countries; but, in the contemporary world, it is primarily a political problem.

Even though a high GNP per capita does not provide a huge margin of productive capacity which can be switched quickly and easily to the production of military strength, the proportion of consumer expenditures which concern neither natural nor acquired necessities, which are therefore discretionary, tends to broaden with rising incomes. And since discretionary spending is more easily postponed by definition, its reduction constitutes a sacrifice which can be effected either voluntarily or by government authority. It is also true that a great deal of fat accumulated in the form of durable consumers' goods facilitates cuts in consumption. But these advantages of a high GNP per capita become significant only if massive increases in military expenditures are called for and cannot be met from an expanding volume of national production.

In general, we can conclude that high rates of income, per capita reflect an economy in which capital is abundant, technology advanced, and labor productivity high, in which education and research are ample and, usually, in which the behavior of entrepreneurs (whether public or private) managers, engineers, scientists, other workers, and consumers favors further economic progress. All of these characteristics indicate valuable resources for the production, deployment and use of technologically advanced weapons; and if present in a large society, constituting a broad as well as rich resource base, they permit the development of great military power. If it is disposed to do so, the high-income nation can provide its military personnel with more and better equipment than can a low-income country from its own resources.

National Economic Growth

National economic growth, reflected in an expanding GNP, results from increases in employment labor and from improved labor productivity which, in turn, may result from investment in capital goods and human resources, economies obtained from a rising scale of production, and especially from technological innovation. As Table 5 illustrates, nations differ greatly in the rate at which their outputs and productive capacities expand; it also indicates that the growth rate of each nation is apt to vary over time.

A steadily growing GNP has a bearing on military economic potential in several ways. The first effect is direct. In nearly all instances, an expanding national income results overwhelmingly from a growing capacity to produce. Whether in any particular case additions to productive factors are specifically suited to the buildup of military strength is an important empirical question which will be further discussed below. In most instances, growing production makes a positive contribution. If, with a GNP of $800 billion, the United States sustains a growth rate of 4 percent per annum, it is adding in one year a margin of production which nearly equals the combined GNP of Sweden and Switzerland.

Second, a rapidly expanding GNP is usually[16] an index of such conditions as an increased supply of labor, capital accumulation, efficient entrepreneurship, technological advance, and improved labor skills, which are resources capable of being tapped for the generation of military forces. To the extent that national income expands on a per-capita basis, and thus reflects economic development, the economy concerned acquires the special advantages associated with a high income per head of the population. A rapidly growing economy in which per-capita income expands persistently is a dynamic economy. It is bound to add to economic military potential. As a nation's economy passes from a lesser to a substantially higher stage of economic and especially industrial development, it will be able to produce more sophisticated military capabilities from its own resources.

A third advantage of an expanding economy, from the viewpoint of military potential, consists of the relative political ease with which new production tasks can be imposed on it, compared with a stationary economy. In a growing economy, more resources can be allocated to the military sector without requiring reductions in the absolute volumes of personal consumption, investment, or other public expenditures. This possibility is illustrated by Table 4 which assumes an economy with a GNP growing at 5 percent a year, and with 10 percent of GNP spent on defense. If the state involved were confronted with the urgent need for a substantial military buildup, its military expenditures could rapidly expand, increasing by almost half

TABLE 4
A Growth Economy with Military Buildup

Year	1	2	3	4	5	6
GNP	100.00	105.00	110.25	115.76	121.53	127.61
Investment	15.00	15.75	16.54	17.47	18.24	19.15
Non-Military Public Exp.	10.00	10.00	10.00	10.00	10.00	10.00
Consumption	65.00	65.00	65.00	65.00	65.00	65.00
Military Exp.	10.00	14.25	18.71	23.29	28.29	33.46

[16]In particular cases, a growing GNP may stem from such conditons as improving terms of trade, and royalties from foreign concerns exploiting the natural resources of the country concerned.

after one year, and by more than 300 percent after five years, even with consumption and non-military public expenditures remaining unchanged, and investment increasing by five percent a year in order to sustain economic growth. A state with a stationary economy, on the other hand, would have to cut consumption and other non-military expenditures in order to double or treble military outlays in real terms.

The point of this particular consequence of economic growth is that it facilitates a military buildup *politically,* other conditions being the same, because the consumer, although he must give up claims to more consumption, is not required to tighten his belt or, in the event of a larger military effort, tighten it as much as in a stationary economy or in one growing only little.

The political and administrative task of government in shifting productive resources to military production may be facilitated by a growing per capita GNP for still another reason. In order to shift resources to the military sector, civilians must either choose not to spend, or lose through inflation, or give up in taxes, a corresponding amount of the purchasing power at their command. In a growing economy with a progressive system of income taxation, unchanged tax rates will yield automatically larger revenues as more taxpayers newly enter income brackets with higher tax rates. To the extent that this happens, no new taxes will have to be imposed by government. Income taxation is more or less progressive in all economically advanced countries, excepting the Communist states.

Some observers have noted that a high and rising national income, though adding to economic military potential, may cause other conditions of national military strength to weaken. Increasing leisure and affluence, it is said, may sap the energies of populations, diminish the integrity of work, undermine the willingness to sacrifice—all qualities which indubitably impinge on military prowess.[17] Does not history know of numerous instances of vigorous, uncouth and economically backward barbarians overrunning centers of incomparable luxury? Yet history also records many cases of rich societies asserting themselves successfully against the onrush of poorer societies. Moreover, the examples of an association between wealth and decay belong to the pre-industrial era. Thus far, there is no evidence that western nations which, over the past three hundred years, experienced an unprecedented rate of economic progress became noticeably decadent as far as the martial virtues are concerned, or that any losses in the physical hardiness characteristic of pre-industrial life were not compensated for by superior logistical capabilities. Such an effect would be in any case immaterial between nations at a similar stage of development. And between highly developed and underdeveloped societies, differences in equipment

---

[17]James R. Schlesinger, "Economic Growth and National Security," *Orbis*, V (Winter 1962), pp. 465–469.

and supplies, education and organization, should go far toward offsetting, if not overwhelming, differences in those military virtues which are supposedly representative of underdevelopment. There may be particular circumstances (*e.g.*, appreciable differences in the uses of increasing wealth and their cultural impact), and there may be special contingencies (*e.g.*, particular theaters of war) which affect the outcome. On the whole, however, it would seem imprudent, at the present stage of knowledge, to regard economic growth as a cause of military decline.

Since economic growth adds to military economic potential, it increases a nation's ability to mount military efforts which demand expanded production, and it facilitates government allocation of more resources to the military sector. As a matter of potential, it made an obvious difference that, from 1962 to 1967, Japan's GNP grew by an average 9.2 percent a year, while the United Kingdom's increased only by an average 3.1 percent.[18] That Japan did not use this expanding potential for military purposes does not matter. What matters is that it could have. Similarly, the fact that the Soviet GNP increased by an average 7.0 percent from 1950 to 1959, whereas that of the United States rose by merely 2.9 percent, made it easier for the Soviet government to manage its military competition with this country, even though the United States had a far larger total product.[19] Table 5 presents growth data for selected countries. Changes for particular countries are as striking as differences between their rates. There is no doubt that the decelerating rate for the Soviet Union put an extra restraint on its military planners.

TABLE 5

Comparative Growth Rates of GNP for Selected Periods[20] (percent)

	1956-61	1962-66	1962-67
Japan	10.9	8.6	9.5
U.S.S.R.	6.4	5.6	5.4
United States	2.1	5.6	5.1
Italy	6.2	5.1	5.0
France	4.9	5.4	4.8
West Germany	6.2	4.3	3.2
United Kingdom	2.9	3.0	3.1

A state with a smaller GNP but higher rate of growth may eventually catch up with one with a higher income but a lower rate of growth. However, it will do so only if the differences in the two rates

[18]U.S. Department of State, Director of Intelligence and Research, Research Memorandum REU–25, May 2, 1968, n.p.
[19]*Ibid.*
[20]90th U.S. Congress, Joint Economic Committee, *Soviet Economic Performance, 1966–1967* (Washington, D.C., 1968), p. 13.

TABLE 6
**Comparative Trends in the Dollar Values of the Soviet and
American GNP's at Market Prices[21]
(billion dollars of 1966 value)**

	1950	1955	1958	1961	1965	1967
United States	414	508	519	575	711	762
U.S.S.R.	132	185	229	272	330	372
Difference	282	323	290	303	381	390
Soviet GNP as % of U.S. GNP	32	36	44	47	46	49

are sufficiently large. The Soviet Union and the United States have
been in this relative position for some time. But as the tabulation in
Table 6 indicates, the slowing down of the Soviet rate in the 1960's,
when the United States rate rose moderately, caused the difference in
total production to increase again after it had been diminishing during
the 1950's.

The Composition of Resources

Economic military potential is determined by the composition of
national resources, and the composition of their growth as well as by
their aggregate magnitude and overall expansion. While the United
States and the Soviet Union, the two outstanding industrial states, are
able to produce every kind of military equipment in their inventories, small and underdeveloped countries, with small industries
mainly manufacturing nondurable consumers' goods, may be able to
import arms and other military supplies, but they are incapable of
producing any but the simplest items from national resources. Indeed,
the vast majority of states are so dependent on foreign military
materiel that this section deals chiefly with the less than twenty
countries which are economically developed and of a size permitting
them to produce at least a substantial portion of their military
hardware.

The kinds of resources required by the military sector depends, of
course, on the type of military effort on which a nation is embarked. It
is one thing to prepare in peacetime for national security. It is another
to be waging war; and if so, the pattern of demands for resources
reflects the scale, character and duration of the conflict. Again, it is
one thing for a state to establish a capability for strategic nuclear
deterrence; it is another to maintain forces for limited war fought
without nuclear weapons, or to prepare forces for intervening in small
local wars, or foreign civil wars, at far distances.

[21]*Ibid.*, p. 16.

The richness of the resource base of states is determined mainly by their economic, and especially their scientific, technological and industrial, development and by the absolute size of the industries peculiarly suitable to the generation of modern military strength. The size of these industries is affected by the proportion of the GNP persistently devoted to producing military capabilities in national enterprises. In these respects, the United States and the Soviet Union are in a class by themselves. Like all other countries, their governments face the fact of ultimate economic scarcity. They also must choose between various desirable configurations of using resources for military and civilian ends. But comparatively speaking, they have been able to turn out an impressive variety of military means in large volume. As we will see, the resource base of other major states—such as Britain, France, and Japan—though dwarfing that of lesser states— is much less rich than that of the superpowers. This is largely, but not wholly, a consequence of lesser scale—a problem discussed in a separate section.

Regarding the *composition* of the national resource base, the military requirements of the large and medium west European powers, and presumably also of the Soviet Union's allies in the Warsaw Pact, are not very different from those of the two superpowers. During the 1950's and 1960's, the main west European countries greatly reduced, if not nearly eliminated, their capabilities for conducting appreciable military operations in other parts of the world, whereas the United States maintained huge capabilities for this purpose and the U.S.S.R., (though its extant capabilities of this kind are still modest), began expanding them at a rapid rate in the middle 1960's. Great Britain and France are maintaining or developing forces for strategic nuclear deterrence, although on a scale vastly smaller than those of the superpowers; and all European military powers of consequence are maintaining "tactical" forces capable of fighting in a nuclear as well as non-nuclear environment. Nevertheless, whatever the differences among their armed forces, the *kinds* of economic resources required by the military sector of all these relatively developed countries is not greatly different. The pattern of resource demand resulting from the military effort of the United States (for which much better data are available than for the U.S.S.R.) may therefore serve as a tolerable way to approach the problem.

Types of Military Expenditures

Table 7 shows a breakdown of United States defense expenditures in terms of operating and capital expenses for selected years. Military personnel costs cover pay, subsistence, transportation, and related expenses for members of the armed services. Operations and maintenance costs cover the salaries of civilian employees and

TABLE 7
Distribution of U.S. Military Expenditures, Fiscal Years 1951, 1960, 1963, 1968
(billions of dollars, percent of total)[22]

Types of Expenditures	1950-51 Amount	1950-51 %	1959-60 Amount	1959-60 %	1962-63 Amount	1962-63 %	1967-68[a] Amount	1967-68[a] %
Operating Expenditures								
Military Personnel Costs	$ 9.3	38.4	$11.7	28.2	$13.3	25.2	$22.00	29.3
Operations and Maintenance	8.6	35.4	10.2	24.4	11.4	21.6	19.1	25.4
Sub-Total	17.9	73.8	21.9	52.6	24.7	46.8	41.1	54.7
Capital Outlays								
Plant Construction	.6	2.4	1.7	4.0	1.2	2.3	2.1	2.8
Equipment Procurement	4.8	20.0	14.7	35.4	17.0	32.0	22.9	30.5
Research and Development	.9	3.8	3.3	8.0	7.2	13.7	7.3	9.0
Sub-Total	6.3	26.2	19.7	47.4	25.4	48.0	32.3	42.3
TOTAL	$24.2	100.0	$41.6	100.0	$52.8[b]	94.8[b]	$75.2[b]	97.0[b]

[a]Official Advance Estimate.
[b]Items for family housing construction, civil defense, military assistance omitted.

consumption-type outlays for such things as office supplies, medical equipment, fuel, and spare parts. Among capital outlays, plant construction involves the building of barracks, airfields, missile launching sites, etc. Procurement is concerned with military hardware, such as aircraft, missiles, ships, tanks, ordnance and ammunition. Research and development is devoted overwhelmingly to hardware invention and development. The distribution of outlays over the different categories varies somewhat among industrial countries and, over time, for each country. There are great differences in the proportion devoted to research and development, with the United States, Britain and France, and presumably the Soviet Union being the top spenders in relation to procurement outlays. The large share of operating expenditures is sensitive, first, to differences in military pay rates, the standard of living afforded to the military, the degree of motorization, etc. It will therefore be higher in the United States and Canada than in Italy or Switzerland. As Table 7 reveals, this share is also sensitive to involvement in war. Thus, in 1950–51, when the United States was waging war in Korea, the percentage was as high as 73.8 compared with 52.6 some years later. The fighting of the United States in Vietnam caused the percentage to rise from 46.8 in 1962–63 to 54.7 in 1967–68. When involved in war, capital expenditures decline proportionately, though they need not, of course, fall absolutely if total military expenditures expand sharply. There is reason to surmise that in time of peace, the distribution of defense expenditure of highly industrialized countries does not differ very much. In the United States, the critical item of procurement outlays has varied between 30 percent and one third in the 1960's. In 1964, it averaged a little over 30 percent in seven European countries (Britain, France, Germany, Italy, Sweden, Holland and Belgium).[23]

Since the goods purchased with operating funds are identical with, or close to, standard commercial items, the resources required for meeting military operations are those utilized in the food, clothing, fuel and similar industries which derive most of their turnover from civilian business. They are typical consumers' goods industries whose output is usually capable of some expansion over the short run, and the consumption of whose products can be rationed in time of emergency. All developed countries have considerable industries of this kind, as they also have construction industries to serve military construction.

[22]Figures for fiscal years 1951 and 1960 from M.L. Weidenbaum, "Problems of Adjustment for Defense Industries," in *Disarmament and the Economy*, eds. Emile Benoit and Kenneth E. Boulding (New York: Harper & Row, 1963), p. 68. Figures for 1963 from U.S. Senate, Hearings before the Subcommittee of the Committee on Appropriations, 88th Congress, *Department of Defense Appropriations for 1964* Washington, D.C., 1963), pp. 114–116. Figures for 1968 from U.S. Senate, Hearings before the Subcommittee of the Committee on Appropriations, 90th Congress, *Department of Defense Appropriations for Fiscal Year 1968* (Washington, D.C., 1967), part I, pp. 3–5.
[23]C.J.E. Harlow, *The European Armaments Base: A Survey* (London: The Institute for Strategic Studies, 1967), P. 1, p. 7.

Military Hardware

It is the procurement of military equipment, and also military research and development, which calls for more special resources. The industries supplying military hardware are primarily the aerospace, electronics, shipbuilding, ordnance, and munitions industries. Their relative importance depends upon the structure of a state's military forces. An emphasis on strategic nuclear deterrence will raise the comparative importance of the aerospace and electronics industries. An emphasis on waging limited tactical war will be expressed in a greater use of the vehicles, ordnance, and ammunition industries and, in the case of a maritime power, of the shipbuilding industry. However, advances in military technology over the past two decades have greatly increased the electronics components of aircraft, ships, and other weapons systems. Involvement in war, depending on its type, will also change the product mix of military hardware produced. For example, table 8 below shows how the composition of ordnance procurement changed in the United States as a result of the wars in Korea and Vietnam. The shift in procurement is certainly very pronounced. It is not surprising that during the Korean War General Motors Corporation, a major producer of tanks and trucks, was the leading military contractor in the volume of orders received, and that by 1960 it had fallen to twentieth place.[24] During the Vietnam War,

TABLE 8
Changes in U.S. Military Procurement[25]

Sophisticated Equipment	Korea	Percent of Total No War	Vietnam
	(Fy 1952)	(Fy 1962)	(Fy 1967)
Aircraft	45.7%	37.7%	39.8%
Missiles	1.4	26.3	8.5
Electronics	4.5	8.4	4.9
Sub-total	51.6%	72.4%	53.2%
Conventional Equipment			
Ships	6.3	12.3	9.8
Ordnance	32.1	12.8	26.4
Other	10.0	4.5	10.6
Sub-total	48.4%	29.6%	46.8%
TOTAL (billions of dollars)	$28.7	$17.9	$24.6

[24]Weidenbaum, "Problems of Adjustment for Defense Industries," in *Disarmament of the Economy,* eds. Benoit and Boulding, *op. cit.* p. 77.
[25]Adapted from *ibid.,* p. 46.

procurement patterns once again exhibited the same tendencies as during the Korean War. The automotive, textile, rubber, and similar industries greatly increased their importance in supplying materiel. Thus, the purchase of clothing went up 240 percent and that of tanks and vehicles by 80 percent.[26]

The comparative importance of product types, and the industries supplying them, as indicated in Tables 9 and 10. The two tables are not strictly comparable. Thus, military research and development outlays are budgeted separately in the United States; also the U.S. table includes outlays on maintenance and operations. Nevertheless, the eminent position of the aerospace and electronics industries is striking in both cases.

The more the primary weapons-producing industries depend on

TABLE 9
U.S. Military Procurement Programs (1963-64)[27]
(millions of dollars)

Program		Program	
Aircraft	$6,070	Fuels	$ 790
Missiles	5,580	Tank-Automotive	750
Electronics	2,920	Ammunition	660
Services	1,800	Subsistence	580
Ships	1,490	Textiles, Clothing	260
Construction	1,360	Weapons	210
Misc. Hard Goods	1,050	All other	2,710

TABLE 10
Military Procurement of Seven European Countries[a] (1964)[28]
(millions of dollars)[b]

Program		Program	
Aircraft	$2,140	Research and Develop.	$1,041
Ordnance and		Ships	880
Ammunition	1,160	Electronics	700

[a]The countries are Britain, France, West Germany, Italy, Sweden, The Netherlands and Belgium. The first three countries accounted for over 80 percent of the total military procurement outlays of the group.
[b]Converted at official exchange rates.

[26]Center of Strategic Studies, *Economic Impact of the Vietnam War*, Special Report Series, no. 5 (Washington, D.C.: Georgetown University, 1967), p. 47.
[27]Adapted from William L. Baldwin, *The Structure of the Defense Market, 1955–1964* (Durham: Duke University Press, 1967), p. 53.
[28]Adapted from Harlow, *op. cit.*, p. 8.

military demand, the less they are capable of expanding output on short notice. The degree of this dependence varies a great deal. It is naturally very small, usually less than 5 percent, for the industries supplying the armed services with maintenance goods such as clothing, food, and fuel. It is extremely high for the ordnance and aerospace industries. In 1964, for instance, 98 percent of the ordnance and 90 percent of the aerospace industries depended on military purchases in the United States.[29] In western Europe, more than two thirds of the aircraft industry turned out military products.[30] In the shipbuilding and electric-equipment industries, the proportion was 60 and 35 percent respectively in the United States in 1964.[31] In Japan, which spends an unusually small proportion of her income on defense, the volume of military aircraft, electronics components, vessels, vehicles and other weapons produced during the mid-1960's accounted for less than 2 percent of the output of the machinery industries.[32]

There has been a strong trend in the United States for a number of giant companies to become very dependent on military demand although they rely on numerous sub-contractors spread over industries themselves less dependent on military orders. These huge concerns—such as General Dynamics and Boeing—are largely in the aerospace industry. Though they are specialists in meeting military demands, they are not highly specialized in the products they manufacture. Most of them make aircraft, missiles, and outer-space hardware, and some are in shipbuilding as well. In fact, staffed with four or five times the number of scientists and engineers than even very innovating companies chiefly serving the private market, with highly skilled personnel coming close to exceeding the number of blue-collar workers, these enterprises are extremely versatile in the product lines they are able to tackle. They are giant complexes of managerial talent, and research and development resources organized for military innovation.[33]

The high skill required in the labor force occupied in the defense industries is illustrated by employment patterns in the United States. Of the nearly 4.1 million civilians engaged in military work for the government or private industry during fiscal year 1967, almost 16 percent were professionals (compared with 13 percent in the general work force), and 21 percent were skilled blue-collar workers (compared with 13.4 percent). The workers who depended most heavily on military spending for their jobs were engineers (18 percent of all engineers employed in the United States), especially aeronautical engineers (61 percent), physicists working in industry (38 percent),

[29]Murray L. Weidenbaum, "Defense Expenditures and the Domestic Economy," in *Defense Management,* ed. Stephen Enke (Englewood Cliffs: Prentice-Hall, 1967), p. 321.
[30]Harlow, *op, cit.,* p. 10.
[31]Weidenbaum, "Defense Expenditures and the Domestic Economy," in *Defense Management,* ed. Enke, *op. cit.* p. 321.
[32]*The Christian Science Monitor,* March 25, 1968, p. 4.
[33]*Cf. Defense Management,* ed. Enke, p. 323; Baldwin, *The Structure of the Defense Market,* p. 95.

electrical and electronic technicians (22 percent), machine-tool operators (19 percent), and metalworking inspectors (24 percent).[34] The proportions should be evaluated in terms of a development, recorded by the Bureau of Labor Statistics, which sees the number of white-collar workers surging past the blue-collar workers in the American labor force.

As far as peacetime military preparations are concerned, and exploitation of the continuously and rapidly evolving technology of modern military strength, these kinds of enterprises which are also found in Europe and Japan, are the key component of military economic potential. Certainly, the industries manufacturing military hardware in time of peace are *the* defense industries. In the contemporary world, potential rests crucially on their size, versatility and innovational capacity; and international comparisons of these industries are the first step toward ascertaining the varying capacity of states for competitive armament.

However, the perspective on economic military potential will broaden if we are concerned with the possibility of intense and prolonged military conflict—although a war not involving the large-scale use of strategic nuclear weapons that would destroy much of the belligerents' population and productive capacity. Under the assumed circumstances, the military sector would claim more than ten or fifteen percent of the national product, the drafting of manpower into the armed forces would be heavy, and the expansion of military production imperative. In other words, nations would be compelled to mobilize a substantially larger proportion of their productive capacity than they do in peacetime or in the event of minor warfare.

Manpower

The larger the military demands made on an economy, the more significant the composition of the population and national productive capacity as a whole. In a prolonged and intensive conflict, the very structure of the population in terms of age groups would be important. The smaller the proportion of the very young and the old—both age groups which are either unproductive or of low productivity—the weaker is the population structure from the viewpoint of military potential. Demographic statistics show the population structures of highly developed countries to be fairly similar. But there are great differences between these states and the economically underdeveloped countries. In the former, the proportion of the very young is moderate but the proportion of the very old is growing as a result of decreasing mortality rates. In the latter, high birth rates and rapid population increase have caused as much as half the population to be under 20 or even under 18 years of age. The following tabulation gives examples of these variations. Of course, in their effect on the size of

[34]Max A. Rutzick, "Worker Skills in Current Defense Employment," *Monthly Labor Review,* (U.S. Dept. of Labor, Sept. 1965), pp. 17–19.

TABLE 11
Population[35]
(percent)

	Age up to 19	Over 64
Venezuela (1965)	55%	3%
Algeria (1960)	52	4
Ghana (1964)	52	2
United States (1965)	39	9
Sweden (1963)	30	12

the working population and manpower draftable into the armed services, the configurations partly offset one another. Statistics show that the population of working age (15-64) in 1961 was between 70.0 and 49.3 percent of the total population in 128 countries. The proportion was relatively high for developed states (*e.g.*, West Germany 67.7 percent, Austria 66.5 percent) and low for underdeveloped states (*e.g.*, Jordan 49.3 percent, Kenya 50 percent). The United States (59.7 percent) and the U.S.S.R. (57.0 percent) were close to the mean.[36]

From a longer-range point of view, differences in the rates of birth and population growth can have considerable repercussions on the comparative potential of states in both categories. Thus, Soviet authorities are reported to be worried about the declining birth rate of the U.S.S.R. From 1926 to 1966, the Soviet birth rate fell from 44 to 18 per 1,000 population, and the rate of population increase decelerated from 2.4 to 1.1 percent over the same period. The Soviet share of the population, which was 8.6 percent in 1940, dropped to 6.9 percent in 1966 and is projected to decline to 5.0 percent by the end of the century.[37] According to projections made by the United Nations, the total population of major regions will grow as follows from 1960 to 1980.[38]

Latin America	78%
South Asia	64
North America	32
East Asia	30
U.S.S.R.	30
Europe	13

[35]Computed from data in United Nations, *Demographic Yearbook 1965* (New York, 1966).
[36]Bruce M. Russet et al., *World Handbook of Political and Social Indicators* (New Haven: Yale University Press, 1964), pp. 25–27.
[37]*The New York Times,* March 24, 1968, p. 14.
[38]United Nations, Department of Economic and Social Affairs, *World Population Prospects As Assessed in 1963,* Population Studies, no. 41 (New York, 1966), pp. 18–20.

Natural Resources

Turning to other resources, the importance of natural resources and of raw materials derived from them is usually exaggerated in the public mind. The dependence of military strength on natural resources has been often overstated, notably in the conception of national *Lebensraum* evolved by the German school of *Geopolitik*. Partly this exaggeration arose because of the belief that war, especially protracted and massive war greatly increases the consumption of raw materials. This is not true. With the exception of a few special materials, materials comsumption has not exceeded normal peacetime requirements in recent wars.[39] But the traditional concern over raw materials and food has been inspired by the fear that dependence on international trade might make a nation vulnerable in time of war. Indeed, a resource structure affording national self-sufficiency in essential foods and raw materials is, even under conditions of prolonged and intensive war, important only if a belligerent country is cut off from foreign sources of supply. However, such wars are not very likely in the contemporary world, and it is equally unlikely that autarchy will be an important asset in future war. In all the wars of the current century, a disruption of vital trade lines has occurred very rarely. The Central Powers were geographically isolated during World War I, but managed to wage a long war of attrition. In World Wars I and II, German submarines for a time threatened an effective blockade of Britain but failed in the end. In the meantime, technological advancement has greatly increased the supply of industrial materials, by adding a large range of man-made synthetics, permitting considerable substitution of one material for another; and, in the case of textile and rubber products, modern inventions have made the northern countries largely independent of the agricultural materials of the tropical and sub-tropical zones. Technological progress has also increased the capability of mining low-grade, and more abundant, mineral deposits. In any event, vulnerability in the sources of foodstuffs and raw materials is hardly an important problem for the two superpowers which are not only richly endowed with natural resources but also possess the military and financial means to draw upon supplies from other countries. Recent advances in agricultural technology have also rendered western Europe as a whole less dependent on outside supplies of essential foods. The great weakness of this region, and of Japan, is their precarious dependence on oil from overseas (mostly the Arab countries). The less developed countries are agricultural. Their former self-sufficiency in essential foods, often cruelly subject to the hazards of weather, has decreased in many cases as growing populations have pressed harder on the means of bare subsistence. Their military hardware is overwhelmingly imported from abroad.

[39]H. J. Barnett, "The Changing Relations of Natural Resources to National Security," *Economic Geography*, XXXIV (July 1958), pp. 193–194.

Generally speaking, there has been and is a trend toward diminishing the importance of land as a factor of production relative to science and technology in military potential. During the first stages of the industrial revolution—crucially based on steam power and iron and steel—leading military powers were eager to develop and secure sources of supply which were invulnerable to enemy action in time of war. By the beginning of the twentieth century, concern over self-sufficiency in food had grown intense, especially among land-locked industrialized countries. But by the late 1960's, rapid technological innovation led to the view that, at least in highly developed economies, land was becoming a factor of production for which capital (*i.e.,* reproducible wealth) could be gradually substituted with growing ease, that is to say, food could be produced with decreasing inputs of land. For many industrial purposes, furthermore, man-made materials produced from abundant rather than scarce natural resources become increasingly substitutable for rarer natural minerals. It should also be noted that lack of local raw materials did not prevent a number of countries from becoming highly developed, industrialized, and wealthy. Thus, without substantial coal and iron deposits, Japan has the world's third largest steel output. She is the second largest manufacturer of automobiles, and has displaced West Germany as the third industrial power in the world. West Germany, Switzerland, Great Britain, and the Netherlands are other examples of advanced economic development despite a niggardly raw materials base.

Industrial Potential

In the event of a major and prolonged mobilization of resources for military purposes, a state's economic potential tends to be the greater (1) the larger manufacturing is a part of total production; (2) the larger the porportion of durable goods (*e.g.,* television sets, refrigerators) in the output of manufactured consumers' goods; (3) the larger the share of capital goods (*e.g.,* machine tools, tractors, railroad cars) in manufacturing; (4) the greater the geographic and occupational mobility of labor; and (5) the greater versatility of factory managements in shifting production tasks. These propositions follow from the facts that the vast bulk of supplies required by the military are manufactures; that durable-goods industries can shift to the production of a large range of military hardware (*e.g.,* from automobiles and ships for the civilian market to motor vehicles and ships for the military); that the capital goods industries cannot only undertake similar shifts (*e.g.,* from tractors to tanks) but also occupy a key role in providing new plants, materials, and machine tools for expanding military production lines; and that labor mobility and managerial versatility obviously facilitate the transfer of workers and work from less to more essential jobs.

A number of service industries are no less essential to military mobilization than manufacturing enterprise. This is eminently true of transportation, electric power generation, and communications. How-

TABLE 12
Contribution of Manufacturing to GNP[40]
(percent)

Malaysia (1964)	9.7%	Japan (1965)	27.2%
Kenya (1965)	11.0	Australia (1964)	28.4
India (1964)	17.0	U.S.A. (1965)	30.6
U.A.R. (1961)	17.4	U. Kingdom (1965)	35.5
Israel (1961)	25.4	W. Germany (1965)	40.9

ever, it may be taken as a general rule that these service industries are developed as a matter of necessity as a country becomes industrialized and generally more developed economically. It is furthermore plausible that labor mobility and managerial versatility grow in response to the same conditions, and are apt to be especially great where the GNP is at least fairly high and, above all, growing persistently and rapidly. Unless a country has extraordinary characteristics to the contrary, therefore, it is possible to limit empirical comparisons to the composition of national output. Statistical materials for such comparisons are readily available.

In order to illustrate international differences along these lines,

TABLE 13
Proportion of Labor Force in Agriculture and Manufacturing[41]
(percent of total labor force)

	Agriculture and Forestry	Manufacturing
Gabon (1963)	84.1%	1.9%
Thailand (1960)	82.0	3.4
India (1961)	72.9	9.5
Ghana (1960)	58.0	8.8
U.A.R. (1960)	56.7	9.1
Mexico (1960)	54.2	13.7
Poland (1961)	47.4	23.3
Finland (1960)	35.5	21.6
U.S.S.R. (1959)	35.2	33.6
France (1962)	19.8	26.9
Argentina (1960)	19.2	25.2
West Germany (1961)	13.4	36.4
Israel (1961)	12.8	21.9
Canada (1961)	12.1	22.9
U.S.A. (1965)	6.2	25.6

[40]Compiled from United Nations, *Yearbook of National Accounts Statistics 1966* (New York, 1967).
[41]Compiled from International Labour Office, *1966 Year Book of Labour Statistics* (Geneva, n.d.).

TABLE 14
Changes in Labor Force Participation
in Agriculture and Manufacturing[42]
(percent of total labor force)

	Agriculture		Manufacturing	
	1960	1965	1960	1965
South Korea	61.9	54.4	6.5	8.6
Philippines	60.5	57.4	9.8	11.6
Spain	41.3	34.5	21.9	24.3
Hungary	38.4	32.7	24.3	26.6
Japan	32.3	26.9	21.7	23.6
West Germany	13.4	10.9	36.4	37.5
Belgium	7.2	5.8	34.7	33.7

Table 12 presents the relative contribution of manufacturing to GNP for some selected countries. Another way to study the relative importance of manufacturing enterprise, and the stage of economic development, is to compare the proportion of national labor forces engaged in agriculture and forestry, on the one hand, and in manufacturing, on the other. Examples are presented in Table 13. The differences in structure are impressive even on the basis of these aggregate data. Equally impressive, as shown by Table 14, is the speed with which these proportions can change in the contemporary world.

It would be interesting to demonstrate the output differences between countries in industries which are close to the production of modern military hardware. While the products of the durable consumers' and the capital-goods industries are not homogeneous enough to permit precise and comprehensive statistical comparisons, some selective comparisons are nevertheless feasible and suggestive. As long as we are interested strictly in the composition of productive resources, these outputs should be related to GNP. The data actually presented in the following simply compare total national outputs, thus reflecting the size of the economy as well as the structure of its output. This is not, however, a practical disadvantage since industrial potential depends in any case on both factors.

From the middle of the nineteenth to the middle of the twentieth centuries, steel production was taken as the key index of industrial military potential. The great steel producers were the great military powers of the world. Although steel has lost this preeminence, it still remains very important in the production of tanks, ships, guns, and other materiel, and also as a vital material for the capital-goods industries. Table 15 records steel production for some selective countries. The two super-powers accounted for 35 percent of world

[42]*Ibid.*

TABLE 15
Crude Steel Production, 1966[43]
(thousands of metric tons)

World Total	45,900	United Kingdom	2,059
United States	10,136	France	1,632
U.S.S.R.	8,075	India	550
Japan	3,982	Turkey	70
West Germany	2,943		

production; together with the next four largest producers, they accounted for 63 percent. The two super powers alone produced 73 percent of the world's primary aluminum in 1965. Japan with 294,000 metric tons being the third largest producer, made less than one-eighth the tonnage of the United States. India produced a mere sixty tons.[44] The following tables on the production of commercial motor vehicles (excluding passenger cars), plastics and resins, and television receivers reveal the same kind of pattern.

If one could have only one index of military economic potential, energy production and consumption would surely rank as the first choice. The data for some selected states appear in Table 19.

From the viewpoint of military potential, the significance of economic growth also derives from the *composition* of the accruing capacity for production. Military potential obviously benefits more from an expansion of the aerospace, electronics, and capital-goods industries than from those turning out more apparel, cosmetics, soft drinks, and comic books. It is therefore important to note international differences in growth as far as industrial production as a whole, rather than the GNP as a whole, is concerned. As Table 20 reveals, although the Soviet GNP increased by about 6 percent a year,

TABLE 16
Production of Commercial Motor Vehicles, 1966[45]
(thousands)

United States	144.0	West Germany	18.0
Japan	120.0	Australia	7.2
U.S.S.R.	69.0	India	2.9
United Kingdom	37.0	Yugoslavia	1.1
France	22.0		

[43]Compiled from United Nations, *Monthly Bulletin of Statistics* (New York, January 1968), pp. 66–67.
[44]United Nations, *Statistical Yearbook 1966* (New York, 1967), p. 302.
[45]United Nations, *Monthly Bulletin of Statistics,* January 1968, pp. 74–75.

TABLE 17
Output of Plastics and Resins, 1965[46]
(thousands of metric tons)

World	14,110	France	695
United States	4,909	Czechoslovakia	124
Japan	2,133	Australia	119
West Germany	1,972	Yugoslavia	57
United Kingdom	957	India	40
U.S.S.R.	802		

TABLE 18
Production of Television Sets, 1965[47]
(selected countries; thousands)

United States	10,036	West Germany	2,776
Japan	4,190	United Kingdom	1,591
U.S.S.R.	3,655	France	1,250

while the American product rose by less than 4 percent, the Soviet volume of industrial, and especially defense-related, production increased much faster than the Soviet GNP. During those years, the Soviet Union made great progress in catching up with the industrial capacity of the United States. If in 1955, the U.S.S.R.'s industrial output was only 34.5 percent by dollar values (or 31.8 percent by ruble values) of American production, by 1963 it had expanded to 77.2 percent by dollar values (68.3 percent by ruble values).[48] This remarkable achievement may well account for the fact that, from 1967 to 1969, the Soviet Union was able to close the gap in intercontinental ballistic missile launchers which had opened up between the United States and itself in the early 1960's.

It is clear from the illustrative data presented in this section that the United States and the Soviet Union are far ahead of all other states in industrial capacity. Their industrial eminence parallels their superiority in the production of military hardware. The United States ranks first in all major branches of production; and if the U.S.S.R. is not second in all cases, the occasional deviation is to be explained by the relatively low Soviet level in the output of specifically consumers' goods. It is also evident that, among the remaining states, the larger industrial countries rank next in industrial military potential: Japan,

[46]United Nations, *Statistical Yearbook 1966*, p. 283.
[47]*Ibid.*, p. 311.
[48]Alexander Tarn, "A Comparison of Dollar and Ruble Values of the Industrial Output of the United States and the U.S.S.R.," *Soviet Studies*, XIX (1968), pp. 484–485.

TABLE 19
Energy Production and Consumption in Selected Countries, 1965[49]
(including coal, lignite, natural gas, crude petroleum)

	Energy Production (million metric tons of coal equivalent)		Energy Consumption Per Capita (Kilograms per capita)
World	5,232	United States	9,201
United States	1,790	West Germany	4,234
U.S.S.R.	929	U.S.S.R.	3,611
United Kingdom	193	France	2,951
West Germany	183	Japan	1,783
India	74	India	172
France	70	Indonesia	111
Japan	62		
Indonesia	36		
U.A.R.	9		

TABLE 20
Soviet Industrial Production Indices[50]

	1955	1960	1963
Official Soviet Index	100	164	212
Total Industry (ruble weight)	100	161	205
Total Industry (dollar weight)	100	167	224
Military and Space-Oriented Output	100	238	461

West Germany, Britain and France, followed at considerable distance by Italy.

Science and Technology

In the modern age, a thriving science and a dynamic technology have become the dominant force in human life. Powerful locomotives of change in the contemporary world, they are the key productive resources affecting all branches of production, civilian and military, and the art of administration as well; it is primarily technological innovation which makes enterprises, industries, and national economies grow in the modern world. The fact that, by the later 1960's, the United States had attained such prominence as an industrial and military power is often attributed to the stupendous increase in its outlays on research and development, which were only $100 million

[49]United Nations, *Statistical Yearbook 1966*, pp. 344–347.
[50]Tarn, *op. cit.*, p. 486.

in 1940, but were scheduled to reach nearly \$17 billion in fiscal year 1968–69. So important had research and development become, and so much had their resource requirements grown, that technological innovation became increasingly a separate activity, giving birth to what has been called the "invention industry."[51] Indeed, just as the process of the industrial revolution led to the industrialization of warfare, so it has, in a manner of speaking, industrialized research and development. This change is manifest in the systematic and massive use of specialized input for a planned technological output, as compared with the previous reliance on the chance of single gifted individuals. As a result, the time lag between discovery and its exploitation has shrunk progressively.[52] In the earlier cases of photography and the telephone, the time lags were 112 and 56 years respectively; in the recent cases of the atomic bomb and the transistor only six or, respectively, five years elapsed.[53]

Technological progress was of course a feature of earlier phases of the industrial revolution. In recent decades, however, it has become more rapid, more continuous and more pervasive. This holds true also for scientific progress which, unlike earlier periods when inventions were largely made by practical men, has become increasingly the basis of technological advance. It is in the distinctly science-based technologies—such as nuclear energy and information processing—that progress has been most spectacular. One aspect of the pervasiveness of scientific and technological advance is that progress in various areas has become inextricably linked with changing technologies quickly acting upon each other. This is an evolution which has led to the interesting concept of technology "transfer space."[54]

Scientific and technological progress boosts military strength in two ways. First and directly, it brings the benefits from innovations in military technology. Second and indirectly, there are the benefits accruing from rapid increases in the productivity of labor and in the productive capacity of national economies, which entails increases in economic military potential. Technological advance is the main root of modern economic growth. It is now generally recognized that the accumulation of intellectual capital in the form of technological knowledge has been a far more copious source of increasing labor productivity than the accumulation of physical capital. As one recent student of the relationship observes, technology is ". . . unquestionably a nation's most important economic resource."[55]

A nation's technological capacity consists of its stock of

[51]Richard R. Nelson, Merton J. Peck, and Edward D. Kalachek, *Technology, Economic Growth and Public Policy* (Washington, D.C.: Brookings Institution, 1967), p. 44.
[52]See the interesting observation on three phases of the industrial revolution in Rober T Gilpin, *France in the Age of the Scientific State* (Princeton: Princeton University Press, 1968), pp. 19–23.
[53]*The New York Times*, Jan. 8, 1968, p. 140.
[54]*Cf.* Erich Jantsch, *Technological Forecasting in Perspective* (Paris: Organization for Economic Cooperation and Development, 1967), pp. 23–28.
[55]Jacob Schmookler, *Innovation and Economic Growth* (Cambridge, Mass.: Harvard University Press, 1966), p. 2.

knowledge of the industrial arts, as diffused through the labor force by means of education, training and work experience, and of its ability to enlarge or enrich this stock by means of research and development. The actual rate at which new technology is generated and diffused depends not only on the supply of productive factors available for research and development, but also, crucially, on the pull of demand for new technology in various sectors of the economy and public life.[56] New technology comes to fruition through the act of innovation, that is, the actual adoption of new production techniques.

The most practical way of comparing the scientific and technological capacity of states is by studying their expenditures on, and their manpower engaged in, research and development (R and D). The pitfalls of such statistical comparison are many. Regarding expenditures, we encounter the usual problem of converting various national expenditures into one currency. If this is done at official exchange rates, the result is unsatisfactory not only because some exchange rates are generally unrealistic in terms of the general purchasing power of the currencies involved, but also because relevant price ratios differ. Thus, American salaries of scientists, engineers and technicians are relatively higher than European salaries. But it is difficult to compute realistic "research exchange rates." There are further problems resulting from international differences in the composition of research tasks; only the United States and the Soviet Union are heavily involved in outer-space technology. Regarding R and D manpower comparisons, difficulties arise from different definitions of engineers and other personnel. As usual, there are special problems in making comparisons with the U.S.S.R. which follows different reporting practices from those of Western countries.[57]

Nonetheless, international comparisons of R and D expenditures and manpower give a rough approximation of differences in national R and D activity and capacity. The following data concern only a selection of the most developed countries. R and D outlays of the underdeveloped countries are comparatively minute.

Table 21 shows gross R and D outlays for a number of countries. United States expenditures are distinctly higher in absolute volume, per capita, and as a proportion of GNP than those of the other countries listed. In fact, the impression of the American lead in expenditures is overwhelming since United States outlays on R and D are nearly ten times those of the United Kingdom, the next largest spender, and about 75 times those of Italy. United States R and D expenditures alone exceeded the entire GNP of such countries as Belgium and the Netherlands. However, since research costs (especially salaries) are higher in the United States than elsewhere, the difference in real inputs is not as great as suggested by Table 21. If one makes allowance for this difference, the United States spent only

[56]*Ibid.*, pp. 199 ff.; Nelson et al., *op. cit.*, p. 28.
[57]All these difficulties are discussed at length in C. Freeman and A. Young, *The Research and Development Effort in Western Europe, North America and the Soviet Union* (Paris. O.E.C.D., 1965), chs. II–V.

between two and three times as much as all European countries together (minus the Communist states), rather than over four times as much as shown in Table 21.[58] This smaller ratio of inputs is confirmed by Table 22 which compares manpower devoted to R and D. On this

TABLE 21
Gross National Expenditures on R and D (1963/64)[59]

	Amount in millions of U.S. dollars at current exchange rates	Per Capita U.S. $	Percentage of GNP At Market Prices	At Factor Costs
United States (1963/64)	21,075	110.5	3.4%	3.7%
United Kingdom (1964/65)	2,160	39.8	2.3	2.6
West Germany (1964)	1,436	24.6	1.4	1.6
France (1963)	1,299	27.1	1.6	1.9
Japan (1963)	892	9.3	1.4	1.5
Canada (1963)	425	22.5	1.1	1.2
Netherlands (1964)	330	27.2	1.9	2.1
Italy (1963)	291	5.7	0.6	0.7
Sweden (1964)	257	33.5	1.5	1.6
Spain (1964)	31	1.0	0.2	0.2
Turkey (1964)	27	0.9	0.4	0.4
Greece (1964)	8	0.9	0.2	0.2

TABLE 22
National Manpower Working on R and D (1962/64)[60]

	Qualified Scientists, Engineers and Technicians	Number per 10,000 of Population
United States (1963/64)	696,500	35.8
Japan (1963)	187,080	19.5
United Kingdom (1964/65)	159,538	29.4
West Germany (1964)	105,010	18.0
France (1963)	85,430	17.8
Italy (1963)	30,280	6.0
Sweden (1964)	16,530	21.6
Spain (1964)	6,480	2.1
Greece (1964)	1,260	1.5

[58]*Ibid.*, p. 33.
[59]Compiled from *The Overall Level and Structure of R and D Efforts in OECD Member Countries* (Paris: O.E.C.D., 1967), p. 14.
[60]Compiled from *ibid.*, p. 14.

basis, it is interesting to note, Japan is ahead of the leading west European states.

From such, not very comparable, data, one concludes that the overall R and D effort of the Soviet Union approximates that of the United States in terms of personnel (see Table 23). In this activity, too, the two superpowers outclass all other states.

In estimating the R and D capability of states, inputs are only a limited and uncertain indicator. One would like to know the comparative productivity of the resources among countries. Thus, the higher American costs of these inputs might or might not be compensated by superior productivity. Unfortunately, the output of R and D defies measurement. Some crude indicators of R and D productivity exist. By comparing international payments for technological knowhow (e.g., license fees, royalties), it is possible to construct a "technological balance of payments." Such calculations reveal that the United States enjoys a hugely positive balance in its relations with other countries—including the advanced European states.[61] For instance, in 1961 transactions with all foreign countries, the United States made payments of $63 million, and received payments of $577 million. In 1963, West Germany received $10 million from the United States, and paid to it $52 million. But the data incorporated in these statistics offer only a very incomplete indicator of R and D productivity. A comparison of patent statistics is even less satisfactory.[62]

TABLE 23
Manpower Engaged in R and D in U.S.A. and U.S.S.R., 1962[63]
(thousands)

	Scientists and Engineers	Other Personnel	Total R and D Personnel per 1,000 population
United States	435.6	723.9	10.4
U.S.S.R.			
Lower Estimate[a]	416.0	623.0	7.3
(Higher Estimate)[a]	(487.0)	(985.0)	(10.4)

[a]It is relatively easy to get data on Soviet R and D manpower in the Academy institutes, the Industrial Research institutes, at the universities and at the level of industrial plants. Great uncertainty exists, however, regarding the personnel in the so-called "Project and Design Organizations" which, on the whole, are not primarily R and D organizations as understood in the West. The lower estimate in Table 23 excludes their personnel, the higher estimate includes half of it. **Cf.** Freeman and Young, *The Research and Development Effort*, pp. 28-29.

[61]Freeman and Young, *op. cit.*, p. 74.
[62]*Ibid.*, pp. 53–54, 75.
[63]Compiled from *ibid.*, p. 72.

TABLE 24
Allocation of R and D Resources between
Different Objectives, 1963/64[64]
(percent)

	Nuclear R and D	Space R and D	Defense R and D	Total 1+2+3	Commercially Motivated	Welfare and miscellaneous
	1	2	3	4	5	6
United States	7	21	34	62	28	10
France	22	1	22	45	41	14
West Germany	8	1	8	17	62	21
Italy	.	.	.	.	73	27
United Kingdom	7[a]	.	33[a]	40	51	9
Norway	7	.	7	14	56	30
Spain	12	.	5	17	64	19

[a]British R and D on military application of nuclear energy is included in Column 3 rather than Column 1.

From the viewpoint of military potential, the distribution of national R and D capacity over various fields of application is of acute interest. Military strength will tend to benefit most from the direct investment of these resources in the advancement of military technology. But efforts in civilian defense-related industries are also important indirectly, even if these R and D efforts are propelled by essentially commercial motivations. Finally, there is a great deal of overlap between the outputs of R and D concerned with the penetration of outer space and direct military R and D. Table 24 shows considerable differences in the distribution of R and D resources even among the most advanced nations. It may be assumed that Soviet use of R and D capabilities is not very dissimilar from that of the United States although commercially motivated R and D probably plays a smaller part in the U.S.S.R. than in the United States. Regarding the other economically advanced states, R and D distribution in Britain and France, both concerned with nuclear weaponry, comes closest to the American pattern. France's large investment in nuclear development reflects her effort to develop independent nuclear armaments. In all countries, but especially in the lesser military powers, the proportion of R and D induced by commercial motivations is strikingly larger than in the United States.

Table 25 presents the distribution, for some selected countries, of R and D resources among three major industries. The comparison reveals that R and D investment in the aerospace industry is small in all countries but the United States, Britain and France. Special historical circumstances account for the lag in Japan and West

[64]From *Overall Level and Structure of R and D Resources, op. cit.*, p. 58.

Germany. All other states have comparative smaller national economies.

Military Research and Development

Although military R and D seems to have an appreciable, although sometimes exaggerated,[65] "spin-off" benefiting technological progress in the production of goods for the civilian market, military technology apparently gains very little from R and D carried on for non-military purposes.[66] Advances in weapons technology are the direct results of military R and D. Internationally, military R and D is even more concentrated in a few states than is all R and D, or R and D which is initiated for the usual commercial reasons.

The economically less developed countries undertake only a miniscule fraction of global efforts in this area of activity. Even most of the highly developed states rely heavily on importing military technology. The United Kingdom pursued a policy of essential self-sufficiency until a few years ago, and Gaullist France is aspiring to such a position at present. But even these countries now import a considerable proportion of the military technology they consume. It is the two superpowers which, engaged in an unrelenting qualitative as well as quantitative arms race, are by far the leading states. Table 26 indicates that, from 1955 to 1965, the United States spent around twice the proportion of its defense budget on military R and D than the main western European powers did; and, in total volume, American R and D outlays were about ten times those of Britain, France and West Germany together. When the United States spent, in the early 1960's, between two and three times as much on all *all* R and D as all

TABLE 25
R and D Effort in Selected Industries and Countries, 1963-64[67]
(percent)

	U.S.A.	U.K.	West Germany	France	Japan	Italy	Norway	Spain	Greece
Aircraft	38.2	28.4	·	22.4	·	·	·	1.2	·
Electrical	19.7	19.8	28.2	26.0	26.0	20.5	16.2	21.7	12.5
Chemicals	12.1	13.2	32.0	17.9	26.2	25.4	16.2	22.2	32.0
TOTAL	70.0	61.4	·	66.3	·	·	·	45.1	44.5

[65]*Cf.* Arnold Kramish, *Atlantic Technological Imbalance: An American Perspective* (London: The Institute for Strategic Studies, August 1967), p. 8.
[66]C.W. Sherwin and R.S. Isenson, *First Interim Report on Project Hindsight*, Summary, (Washington, D.C.: U.S. Department of Defense, Office of the Director of Defense Research and Engineering, June 30, 1966; revised Oct. 13, 1966), p. 12.
[67]*Overall Level and Structure of R and D Resources, op. cit.*, p. 58.

TABLE 26
Military R and D of four selected countries, 1955-65[68]
(annual average, millions of dollars)

	Defense Expenditures	Military R and D Outlays	R and D as a percentage of Defense outlays
United States	$48,500	$5,300	11.9%
United Kingdom	4,500	205	5.5
France	3,600	250	6.9
West Germany	3,500	85	2.5

west European countries together, in military R and D the United States outspent the western European countries by a ratio of 7:1 (if outlays are converted at official exchange rates), and by a ratio of 4:1 or 5:1 (if a "research exchange rate" is used in order to allow for higher American costs).[69] While comparable data for the Soviet Union are lacking, it is assumed that its military R and D outlays are on a scale approaching that of the United States.[70] This gross international imbalance is paralleled *within* western Europe. Of all military R and D spending in Europe in 1962 and 1964, over 95 percent was spent in Britain, France, West Germany, Italy, Sweden, the Netherlands and Belgium; and Britain and France accounted for about 85 percent of all military R and D expenditures of this group of countries.[71] The fact is that, at this time, only two states—the United States and the U.S.S.R.—can afford to stay at the forefront of the military technology concerned with strategic military power. In this area of weapons technology in particular, their keen competition induces these countries to move boldly without close regard to costs. This inducement follows from the fact that technological superiority in military, and especially in key strategic systems, is a far more overriding objective than such superiority usually is in competitive markets for civilian goods.[72] This means that military R and D is pressed with a lesser sensitivity to costs and risk than is the case with other kinds of R and D. Technical excellence is regarded as central to military strength. As between the two superpowers, indeed, foreging ahead in military R and D has become *per se* an important component of military power. It may not always be necessary to *produce* the new military systems that have been developed provided the fact of their development, and the possibility of their procurement is known to, and appreciated by the rival power.[73] The significance of national scientific and tech-

[68]From Kramish, *op. cit.,* p. 6.
[69]Freeman and Young, *op. cit.,* p. 34.
[70]*Ibid.,* p. 35.
[71]Harlow, *op. cit.,* p. 19.
[72]Baldwin, *op. cit.,* p. 112.
[73]*Ibid.*

nological potential, like all components of military potential, depends upon the uses military power and the types of situations in which it is employed. It is most important in providing the means for deterring other states from using military power with a high technological content, as in strategic nuclear deterrence, but in the future conceivably also in the deterrence of military attack featuring exotic technologies. It will tend to be of least consequence in situations— such as counter-guerrilla operations in economically underdeveloped areas with physically forbidding terrain—in which various geographical and political conditions restrict the use of technologically sophisticated military systems. However, even in such situations there is always an appropriate technology, suited to the structure of limitations, which can be developed, provided there is time, and whose availability will *per se* favor the military power in a position to employ it. A national capacity for dynamic military technology, in other words, can be applied to a vast variety of challenging circumstances. It is only that many developed technologies, very sophisticated and expensive, are specialized and hence closely restricted to particular uses. They do not have to be, and are not, designed for much versatility. The evolution of technologically rich weapons thus suggests the difference between the general-purpose tool, including the general-purpose machine tool, which dominated industrial production until the early part of the present century, and the sophisticated special-purpose machine tools which, having been developed in ever-increasing variety, dominate contemporary industrial production. A nation with a rich base in science and technology is able to produce a range of sophisticated weapons which *together* lend versatility across the board and which, for each type of military situation, can give its possessor a distinct advantage, everything else being the same.

The concentration of large scientific and technological resources in the leading states on developing military technology make it, of course, possible for these nations to invent and deploy ever more powerful means of destruction which, if used in unrestricted war, threaten to extinguish entire nations and quite possibly the human race.[74] Yet—ironically enough—as the history of nuclear weapons has already intimated, actual combat with technologically sophisticated arms of mass destruction has become obviously unproductive on behalf of any rational configuration of national objectives when their use is reciprocal and defenses against them are inadequate. And their employment against technologically inferior states is becoming increasingly restrained by political and moral considerations. These restraints may fail to prevent the employment of such weapons, but they reduce the likelihood of their use, and may well do so to an extent that their employment will come about only inadvertently.

---

[74]Cf. *Unless Peace Comes: A Scientific Forecast of New Weapons*, ed. Nigel Calder (New York: Viking Press, 1968).

Since their possessors are on guard even against this contingency, the probability of inadvertant use is accordingly smaller than the previous history of warfare would seem to suggest.

To the major powers—particularly to the United States and the U.S.S.R.—R and D on such armament, and on further military inventions, remains an essential condition of great-power status as long as the present international system, with the organization of coercive means left to the discretion of nation-states, prevails. Without general and comprehensive disarmament, deterrence of possible attacks with weapons of extremely massive destruction means a valid objective of government, and so does apparently the development of still more powerful arms, even though their use would be senseless. But, as already indicated, modern capabilities for military R and D can also be directed toward making arms for limited forms of warfare more sophisticated. Sophistication does not necessarily mean more massive destruction of human life. It could also mean achieving military objectives efficiently in other terms, *e.g.,* with increased speed, and conceivably even minimum destruction of life and property. The past direction of military R and D has been guided perhaps unimaginatively by traditional concepts which, established under conditions of a relatively primitive technology, made an increase in the deadliness of weapons the prime objective. These traditional concepts may be obsolete in the present age of technology. They certainly look that way.

The Technology Gap

The leading European nations, which were in the forefront of scientific and technological advance until World War II, have become shocked of late by the huge technology gap which seems to have opened between Europe and the United States. The vaulting anxiety has become only sharpened by large direct investments of American industrial firms in western Europe,[75] and by the so-called "brain drain," that is, a persistent net migration of European scientific and engineering talent of the United States. This country has been accused of technological imperialism and British Prime Minister Harold Wilson has expressed the fear that Europe would be doomed to an "industrial helotry" unless effective countermeasures were taken.[76] Contrary to many exaggerated statements, the American technological superiority of the 1960's does not extend across all fields of innovation. It is striking in the aerospace industry and in electronics, especially the computer industry; but European technological accomplishment surpasses the American in shipbuilding and roughly equals it in the automobile industry and in many branches of the chemical and metallurgical industries. Nevertheless, evidence of an

[75]For example, U.S. direct investments in France increased from $217 million in 1950 to $1,584 million in 1965; Gilpin, *op. cit.,* p. 45.
[76]*Ibid.,* ch. I.

overall technological discrepancy is overwhelming. European concern over it has stimulated attempts to explain the causes of the gap, and thereby lay bare the conditions for rapid and broad technological progress.

The fact that the technological strength of western Europe does not at present match its general industrial performance and its economic prosperity reflects no doubt the effects of World War II, which saw Europe's industrial and technological capacity in large part run down, if not destroyed outright. Following the war, the pent-up demand for consumers' goods and services induced European governments and industries to neglect the rebuilding of technological prowess at a time when their intense political, ideological, and military rivalry motivated Soviet and American authorities to press technological advancement on a broad front.[77]

Among the specific hypotheses advanced for explaining the "technology gap," the following seem to be interesting. They are at least plausible in pointing to contributing factors. But the relationships between the conditions on which they focus is not well enough understood, and there is no adequate knowledge permitting the distribution of weight over the variables concerned.

One thesis, favored by many observers, is that the American managerial class, private and public, is more eager to innovate and more adept at innovation than its European counterparts,[78] although, of course, marked differences exist in both regions between different branches of industry, government and other institutions, such as the universities. Innovation is an act essentially different from invention, or the creation of new knowledge. The innovator is an entrepreneur who decides to apply new knowledge—a new technique, commodity or service—once it is available. He invests capital in the innovating act, envisions new needs for new technology and is prepared to adapt existing organizations to the demands of innovation. Thus, innovation requires risk-taking and resourceful management.[79] It demands both appropriate attitudes and skills. Concerning attitude, the modern innovator not only eagerly awaits opportunities for innovation, but also creates these opportunities by investing in R and D. Many observers believe that American management on the whole is more disposed than the European managerial class to want, recognize, encourage, reward and exploit technological creativity. Although western European countries have ample resources for basic and applied research, these are not adequately appreciated by many managers who are often technologically unsophisticated and hidebound. Even in Britain, where the volume of R and D expenditures is comparatively large, innovation is often lagging and haphazard, and

[77]Alastair Buchan, *The Implications of a European System for Defence Technology* (London: Institute for Strategic Studies, October 1967), p. 3.
[78]*Cf.* John Diebold, "Is the Gap Technological?," *Foreign Affairs,* XLVI (January 1968), pp. 276–291; Edward G. Moline, "Das Problem der 'technologischen Lücke' zwischen den Vereinigten Staaten und Europa," *Europa-Archiv,* XXII (June 1967), pp. 427–434.
[79]Nelson et al., *op. cit.,* pp. 97–108.

therefore fails to engender all its potentially positive effects on productivity.

But successful innovation turns on managerial skills as well as motivation. R and D efforts must be efficiently selected and proportioned, and repeated screening is important as the process of development demands more funds. Commerically motivated innovation involves careful market studies, product design, and sales efforts. For the propagation of these skills, the kinds of higher business training favored and available in the United States may be a key factor in American success; and for the evolution of these skills, the development of new managerial techniques, such as systems analysis, may themselves have been extremely valuable innovations.

Second, technological innovation will tend to flourish in proportion to the funds spent on basic and applied research, and on development; and it also tends to prosper in proportion to the rewards conferred on scientists, engineers, and other R and D personnel. The allocation of funds for this purpose depends, of course, on the level of national income and is facilitated by a steadily expanding income. But it depends also on the values of those whose positions in government, industry and universities give them influence on the allocation of resources. A managerial class which is avid for innovation is apt not to begrudge money for even very riskful R and D. Even in states favoring private enterprise, the supply of public funds is crucial in this connection because expected and actual private returns to invention and innovation will fall far short of the social returns over the larger sections of the scientific and technological frontier. External economies are decisive in the pursuit of pure science, in military R and D, and in other technologies of special interest to the public sector. Unquestionably, scientific and technological progress in the United States expresses both a huge increase in total R and D funds over the past three decades, and the striking appearance of public largess. In 1965, for example, about 70 percent of all R and D moneys originated with the federal government. But R and D has become largely "nationalized" also in the West European countries, and is of course constitutionally so in the Communist states. Regarding the matter of personal incentives, it is assumed that the 4,868 scientists and engineers who emigrated to the United States between 1956 and 1961, almost half of them from Europe, were attracted by higher salaries, quicker advancement, and better research facilities.[80]

Nations also differ in the efficiency with which R and D funds are spent. For example, Japan ranks very high in terms of technological advance. This is in keeping with a large employment of manpower on R and D (see Table III–22) but is in remarkable contrast to the relatively modest expenditures made on R and D. These outlays have been only

[80]*Cf.* Freeman and Young, *op. cit.*, pp. 57–59, 76.

a very small fraction of United States spending for this purpose. Japan's success with innovation has been achieved with remarkable efficiency. Its imports of technology have also been large.

Third, while the demand for new knowledge and technological innovation is probably the strategic variable in stimulating and expanding these activities, and though a strong and persistent demand induces the supply of inputs to grow in the long run, in the short run the availability of these resources is a governing condition. The key resources are a growing stock of basic scientific knowledge and educated and trained personnel.

The evolution of modern technology is increasingly related to scientific advance. It is in fact science-based invention and innovation which permits a succession of radical technological advances;[81] and the development of a rich national science base has therefore become a prerequisite of technological leadership. In this respect, "basic science"—the unfettered search for new knowledge for its own sake—is ultimately the foundation on which a flourishing applied science has come to rest. Indeed, all the great industrial countries are deeply engaged in cultivating pure science as well as applying new knowledge to practical ends on a massive scale. Everywhere in modern nations, research has gained in scope, variety, funding, prestige, and exploitation. To be sure, the presence of first-rate scientists does not insure technological innovation; but—as the examples of molecular biology, solid-state physics, plasma physics, and econometrics testify—a bold outward push across the technological frontiers is impossible in their absence.

The increased relevance of science to such progress has emphasized the importance of formal education, especially graduate study. Regarding the "technology gap," it seems therefore relevant that over 40 percent of all college-age youths in the United States are enrolled in higher education compared with, for instance, 15 percent in France, and 7 percent in West Germany and Italy.[82] It has been estimated that, including the value of educational activities not normally included in national product statistics, the United States spent $60 billion, or approximately 13 percent of its GNP, on education in 1957–58,[83] and it is certain that this proportion has increased. On the whole, educational expenditures in western Europe are only half of the American.[84] On the other hand, it has been observed that Japan's remarkable postwar success in economic and technological growth is closely related to her heavy investment in formal education. As many as 70 percent of Japanese children, compared with 40 percent in Britain, continue their schooling to the

[81]Nelson et al., *op. cit.*, p. 40.
[82]Moline, *op. cit.*, p. 432.
[83]Fritz Machlup, *The Production and Distribution of Knowledge in the United States* (Princeton: Princeton University Press, 1962), p. 107.
[84]Moline, *op. cit.*, p. 431.

age of eighteen and beyond; and some sixteen percent, versus ten percent in the United Kingdom, go on to college or university.[85] Soviet data are unfortunately not comparable. It has been estimated, however, that the median of school years for the Soviet population is sixteen years and older, increased from 5.9 in 1960 to 6.6 in 1965. The comparative numbers for the United States are 10.9 and 11.9.[86]

The accompanying table shows numbers of graduate students for several selected countries. Owing to different definitions and practices, these data must be interpreted with considerable caution. The information for Mainland China looks dubious. But the table does bring out differences of an order of magnitude which are significant. As one would expect, the highly developed countries have the most graduate students when numbers are related to size of population. As within countries, among countries the rich can afford the most education.

Quantitative data of this kind present only one dimension of national educational performance. The quality of educational systems is the other dimension. There are, of course, differences in the competence of teachers to evoke student interest, to transmit knowledge, and to instill the quest for new knowledge, pure or applied. By and large, formal education in all the highly developed societies is

TABLE 27

Graduate Education, Selected Countries, 1960-63[87]

(thousands of enrolled students)

	Total	Natural Sciences	Engineering
United States (1963)	614.2	74.9	47.5
China (Mainland) (1962)	220.0	10.0	77.0
Japan (1963)	185.8	4.6	28.5
India (1960)	179.0	n.a.	8.0
France (1962)	70.9	20.8	6.2
United Kingdom (1962)	67.3	10.7	17.9
West Germany (1962)	58.0	3.1	18.9
Italy (1962)	24.0	3.2	2.4
UAR (1963)	20.9	1.3	2.1
Brazil (1963)	18.5	.7	2.0
Australia (1962)	14.8	1.3	1.8
Sweden (1962)	6.7	1.0	1.0
Ghana (1963)	1.8	--	--

[85]Cf. "Seven Keys to the Sun," in "The Risen Sun," *The Economist* (London), May 27–June 7, 1967, p. x.
[86]90th U.S. Congress, Joint Economic Committee, *Soviet Economic Performance, 1966–67* (Washington, D.C., 1968), p. 81.
[87]United Nations Educational Scientific and Cultural Organization, *Statistical Yearbook* (Mayenne, France, 1966), pp. 326–388.

competitive, examination-controlled and, in this sense, achievement-oriented. This is precisely what is wanted for the underpinning of scientific and technological advance. The more universities become differentiated structures which produce expertise in large numbers of young people, the better they function from this point of view. (It is a point of view, however, against which some students have been rebelling during the mid-1960's at American and European universities, because this orientation neglects other possible functions of education.) Regarding formal education as a basis for technological progress, it is also important that training in engineering, business administration, and applied research be accorded as much social prestige as education in the basic sciences and other professional fields such as medicine and the law. This is definitely not the case in Britain, France, and other European countries, and still less so in many underdeveloped countries. This partiality is much less pronounced in the United States and Japan.

Fourth, larger institutional and cultural factors, which are less clearly understood in their effects, probably have an important impact on the R and D capability of nations. Institutional arrangements concern particularly relations between the R and D-related activities of government agencies, manufacturing enterprises, universities, and non-university research institutes. The bulk of R and D funds come from the public purse in all industrial countries, but there are substantial differences in the institutions which receive these funds. Great Britain, for example, chose major reliance on government laboratories rather than on private enterprise. In fact, its institutional arrangements for promoting and conducting R and D have undergone frequent changes since World War II, indicating a lack of satisfaction with the results achieved, and it is not clear that the present regime is conducive to vigorous innovation.[88] The Soviet Union has also concentrated its major research effort on special institutes; only 2 percent of Soviet research staffs work in industrial enterprises, compared with about 60 percent in the United States.[89] Even though the bulk of American R and D funds are public, actual research is extremely decentralized, and the federal authorities grant a high degree of discretion in the use of these monies.[90] The United States has been inventive in creating a large variety of laboratories, some connected with major universities (e.g., The Lincoln Laboratory at the Massachusetts Institute of Technology, and the Lawrence Radiation Laboratory at the University of California); some as non-profit institutions outside the universities (such as the RAND Corporation, the Brookhaven National Laboratory, and the Battelle Memorial Institute);

[88]Cf. Alan G. Mencher, "Management by Government: Science and Technology in Britain," *Bulletin of Atomic Scientists*, XXIV (May 1958), pp. 22–27.
[89]*Soviet Studies*, Information Supplement, (University of Glasgow, January 1968), p. 16.
[90]Cf. Gilpin, *op. cit.*, pp. 132–138; also see the conclusions of a European study (O.E.C.D.) as reported in *The New York Times*, January 13, 1968, p. 10.

others under direct public auspices (such as the Naval Ordnance Test Center and the National Bureau of Standards); and still others operated by private firms on government contract (*e.g.,* the Sandia Corporation). There is general agreement that the American R and D enterprise benefits from a close rapport and highly flexible arrangements among government, industry, and universities. Despite a very pluralistic constitution of the R and D enterprise, there is a great deal of effective coordination.

National R and D performance is also affected by the larger cultural context. Deep and continuous changes in commercial, occupational, and educational patterns must occur in a society in which scientific and technological innovation abounds. Radical innovation on a broad front involves a vast learning process for government, workers, and consumers.[91] It will not take place where resistance to such change is strong. It will happen where there is far-reaching consensus on the value of innovation and the net utility of innovation-induced change. This vital component in national R and D capacity was described eloquently by a European committee of experts concerned with the R and D gap between western Europe and the United States:

All the driving forces of American society have been marked with a scientific orientation and all the skills have been mobilized. The major goals set by the responsible leaders are no longer challenged; that is perhaps the most striking thing to European observers. The scientific and technological effort is therefore deployed in an almost total consensus.

In the last analysis, the secret of success no doubt lies there, in this common determination to pursue the same enterprise, the aim of which is change . . . .

We looked in the United States for a science policy; in fact there are many. But what we did find, in the formulation, implementation and achievement of these policies, is first and foremost a convergence of interests and motivations to construct the future; the adventure of scientific and technical research appears as the main way of success to this future in which the drive and ambitions shown by a whole nation will be expressed.[92]

This panegyric perhaps exaggerates cultural and institutional receptiveness to innovation, which is extremely upsetting of institutional life, and subversive of the degree of order and routine which is also a prerequisite to achievement in business and government. Rapid innovation, therefore, provokes resistance anywhere, including the United States.[93] But the resistance is less insistent there than in most, if not all, other industrial states. A strong dedication to progress, along with the reach of formal education, accounts for the remarkable mobility of the factors of production in science and technology in the United States. Technological progress is a matter of

---

[91] Nelson et al., *op. cit.,* pp. 97–108.
[92] *The New York Times,* January 13, 1968, p. 10.
[93] See the Penetrating analysis in Donald Schon, *Technology and Change* (New York: Delacorte Press, 1967).

cultural development and adaptation.[94] This is one condition which slows down the international distribution of a thriving R and D spirit. Techniques can be easily communicated in the modern world, but only when the recipients understand and accept the consequences of adopting new technologies. It is hard to import culture.

Finally, there is a more technical condition which indubitably accounts in considerable part for the present American R and D superiority over the western European states. This is the factor of scale. Many of the newly emerging technologies require a scale of application, and a scale of effort even in their nascent stage, which goes beyond the resources that single European countries—and not only the smaller ones—can afford. This factor is discussed in the following section (see pp. 90–92).

However, the American capability is not without flaws. For instance, the United States has a strong penchant for embarking on big prestige projects; federal funds for basic science are not nearly as easy to obtain as for applied research. The practice of *ad hoc* funding of research projects has deciced weaknesses which show up particularly in the support of basic research. Much of the time of top scientists is absorbed by efforts to secure funds;[95] the social sciences have been relatively neglected by public authorities; more recently the upward curve of R and D money has been flattening out or becoming less steep, in part in response to the fiscal stringencies caused by the war in Vietnam.

Major European countries, now acutely worried about the gap between them and the U.S., are making strenuous efforts to reduce it. Whether and to what extent they will succeed is a matter of the future. There are so far no signs of a narrowing of the gap; and some observers predict that it will widen further. One of these observers believes that a pioneering United States is becoming a "technetronic" society which is "becoming shaped culturally, psychologically and economically by the impact of technology and electronics, particularly computers and communications,"[96] and that this metamorphosis will increasingly separate this country—"*the* creative society" of this age—from the rest of the world.

Conclusion

Beyond doubt, for the major powers, and for the production of most forms of military strength in the modern world, a nation's scientific and technological potential, not its stock of raw materials, is

[94]Joseph Ben-David, "The Scientific Role: The Conditions of its Establishment in Europe," *Minerva*, IV, 1965, pp. 15–54.
[95]*Cf.* Daniel S. Greenberg, *The Politics of Pure Science* (New York: The New American Library, 1967).
[96]Zbigniew Brzezinski, "America in the Technetronic Age," *The Atlantic Community Quarterly, VI (Summer 1968), p. 175.*

the key factor. The Weizmann Institute is a far more valuable asset to Israel than would be sizeable coal deposits. In fact, the potency of R and D capabilities is likely to grow as further innovation is applied to the invention and innovation processes themselves. One of the next advances on the horizon in this direction is that the development of more sophisticated information systems will permit the creative power of the most gifted engineers to be greatly amplified.[97]

The main bases of national R and D capabilities are three. One is the urge to create and apply new knowledge firmly represented in government, industry, and universities; and the accompanying disposition of societies to adapt to the unsettling consequences of innovation. The second is the supply of capital, for the application of new technology requires a great deal of investment, a fact which inevitably lends an advantage to nations which are rich and enjoy a copious rate of capital formation in human as well as in inanimate resources. The third are economies of scale which, in respect to some very demanding technologies, favor nations which are large as well as highly productive.

The Factor of Scale

One factor which the Soviet Union and the United States, leading in military R and D by an enormous margin, have plainly in common is sheer size—the scale of their industries, the volume of their capital formation, and the level of their R and D expenditures. They dwarf all other countries in nearly all the relevant quantitative indices. This kind of advantage operates, of course, also among the other states. It favors the United Kingdom and France over Belgium or Austria; and it gives all economically very advanced societies an advantage over underdeveloped countries of comparable population size.

Regarding economic and technological potential for military strength, a large scale is beneficial in two ways. First, over an extensive range of manufacturing industries and enterprises, and R and D enterprises as well, there tend to be substantial "internal" and "external" economies of scale which diminish unit costs of production and thus enhance factor productivity. Internal economies, which are derived from the expansion of individual enterprises, result mainly from the fact that some productive factors are indivisible and/or specialized, their use becoming possible or profitable only if the volume of output is sufficiently large. External economies, derived from the growth of industry in general, stem from a large supply of labor of various skills, of specialized services and products, etc., on which individual enterprises can draw.

National economies which are of continental size, and highly

---

[97]*Cf.* Ford Park, "Tomorrow's Engineer," *Science and Technology,* no 72 (December 1967), pp. 20–34.

industrialized, afford these advantages to many of their industries and enterprises, thereby increasing their industrial military potential by some margin. It is, however, in the specific way that national scale directly benefits the production of advanced military technology, which is much the more important. Some objects of research, development and production are so demanding in their financial and other requirements that even highly developed countries of the size of France or West Germany do not afford a large enough national base. This is the case with such projects as developing a new supersonic airplane, outer-space craft, or a sophisticated computer industry, or an anti-ballistic missile defense. These kinds of project demand huge funds and large combinations of highly specialized and expensive manpower and equipment. National differences in resource supply is crucial in such cases whether one looks at entire industries or individual firms. In 1966, for example, the seven leading west European countries together had a total employment of 440,000 people in their aerospace industries, whereas the United States alone employed 1,400,000.[98] In 1963–64, the average R and D expenditures per company of the twenty largest firms was $1.414 million in the United States, $132 million in Britain, $65 million in France, and $27 million in Italy.[99]

These data do not mean that states of the size and wealth of Britain and France are unable, on their own, to organize some very big development projects. But they are unable to pursue many and must be severely selective. Indeed, by means of intelligent selection, a nation as small as Sweden has achieved impressive results in designing and producing some very sophisticated armaments.[100] But the need to be severely selective puts these middle powers in a class appreciably inferior to the U.S.S.R. and the United States. And the types of projects which pose a very high threshold of absolute expenditures fall within military and space technology, and in electronic informaion technology which is essential to complex military systems. Within the United States the advantages of scale are pronounced in these industries.[101] Moreover, to this size requirement on the resource side must be added the size of the markets for the products of these industries. These markets are huge in the United States, but they are necessarily much smaller in countries such as Britain and France.[102] No wonder it is widely assumed that no single European state has the scale of resources demanded by very complex systems in the military and outer-space fields or at least a scale of resources to aspire to first-rank military power.

[98]Buchan, *op. cit.,* p. 3.
[99]*The Overall Level and Structure of R and D Efforts, op. cit.,* p. 62.
[100]*Cf.* Harlow, *op. cit.,* pp. 2–3, 7–8; Herbert Büchs, "Rustungszusammenarbeit in der NATO als Mittel zur Einigung der technologischen Lucke, *Europa-Archiv,* XXII, November 10, 1967, p. 704.
[101]Baldwin, *op. cit.,* pp. 115–117.
[102]*Cf.* Buchan, *op. cit.,* p. 4.

It is not surprising, therefore, that alarmed Europeans have explored the possibility of consolidating west European resources in order to attain the advantages of large scale and create the foundation for technological independence. If the members of the European Common Market (France, West Germany and the Benelux countries) and Britain could be integrated into one uniform economic, political, and military system, the resulting combine would command resources and a potential for military power comparable to that of the superpowers. In 1966, their aggregate population was 236 million, compared with 233 million in the U.S.S.R. and 197 million in the United States. In the same year, their production of steel was 9.1 million tons against 10.0 million tons in the United States and 8.1 million in the Soviet Union; and their monthly electricity output was 52.7 million kwh compared with 104.0 million in the United States and 45.4 million in the Soviet Union.[103]

Yet even though the present industrial and technological inferiority of western Europe poses the question of whether the dimensions of the traditional nation-state are adequate for developing and managing the immense, complex technologies bred by modern science,[104] this does not, of course mean that the political preconditions for western European integration are present or will emerge. Measures short of what would amount to federation are likely to permit only modest success in dealing with the problem of insufficient scale. So far, cross-national business cooperation and inter-governmental programs on R and D have encountered discouraging obstacles. Also, merely creating a common market may not help very much. At least thus far, it is American enterprises, accustomed to large-scale enterprise, and possessing a superior array of management skills, which have taken main advantage of operating expansively in the European Common Market. Perhaps European firms will adjust themselves in time to the new market scale, particularly if legal, financial and political impediments are removed. In the meantime, there are plenty of ideas for European (and cross-Atlantic) cooperation in the defense field.[105] It remains to be seen whether or not such ideas to overcome the handicap of inadequate scale will prove feasible.

The Economically Less Developed States

According to the foregoing analysis, the economically underdeveloped countries have, as a class, only an extremely small, if any, economic and technological potential for developing sophisticated military capabilities, even excepting nuclear forces. This inferior status is the direct result of small GNP's, weak industrial capacities,

[103]Data from United Nations, *Monthly Bulletin of Statistics,* January 1968, pp. 1–4, 66–67, 86–89.
[104]Gilpin, *op. cit.,* p. 4.
[105]*Cf.* Buchan, *op. cit.,* pp. 12–13; Büchs, *op. cit.,* pp. 708–710.

TABLE 28
Military Jet Aircraft Imported[a] by Selected Countries, 1955-65[106]
(numbers)

UAR	450	Philippines	80
Iraq	124	Ethiopia	20
India	558	Argentina	105
Pakistan	192	Brazil	80
Indonesia	115	Cuba	220
Thailand	112	Mexico	35

[a]Some aircraft produced on license.

TABLE 29
Sources of Major Weapons in Selected Countries, 1945-65[107]

Recipient Country	Jet Aircraft	Missiles	Warships	Tanks
UAR	USSR	USSR	USSR, GB	USSR, GB, Fr.
Iran	US	US	GB	US
India	USSR, GB, Fr.	USSR	GB	USSR, GB, Fr., US
Pakistan	US, W. G.	US, WG	GB, US	US, China
Indonesia	USSR	USSR, Fr.	USSR, Italy	USSR, Fr.
Argentina	GB, Fr., US		GB, US	US
Cuba	USSR	USSR	US	USSR

Note: GB = Great Britain; Fr. = France; WG = West Germany.

and usually the absence of any significant capacity for scientific and technological advance.

These characteristics do not of course imply that countries in this class have no military potential or military power whatever. First, they enjoy such potential regarding military conflicts with neighboring states of similar economic capacity. Second, there are marked differences in the state of economic development, and in the current rate of economic growth, achieved by these countries. Although as a group their economic military potential may look completely outclassed by that of the highly industrialized states, North Korea is in this respect much superior to Cambodia, or Pakistan to Afghanistan, or the U.A.R. to the Sudan, or Argentina to Paraguay, etc. Third, the less developed countries are able to import modern military technology in the form of weapons and military advice and training.

[106]Adapted from John L. Sutton and Geoffery Kemp, *Arms to Developing Countries, 1945-1965*, Adelphi Papers, No. 28 (London: Institute for Strategic Studies, October 1966), pp. 36–37.
[107]*Ibid.*, p. 45.

Fourth, they may have considerable potential for military encounters with industrially far superior states provided there are conditions compensating for the forms of military strength that are characteristic of industrial states. Fifth, as among the industrialized nations, size and scale makes a difference among the less developed countries. This factor, for example, greatly favors Mainland China and India as military powers in Asia, and Brazil and Argentina in South America. Since these factors can be additive, large and populous countries which have made and are making considerable economic and industrial progress, and which are able to import military supplies and assistance on a large scale, have the makings of a very substantial military power in their geographic region.

The first two points of qualification are so obvious as to need no further discussion. But the last three deserve clarification.

Arms Imports

A number of less developed countries have a capability to manufacture simple arms, and a few (*e.g.,* India) produce more complicated weapons, usually on license from one of the industrialized states. But the bulk of modern military systems—aircraft, missiles, tanks, and ships—maintained in the economically less developed world has been imported from abroad. The chief exporting nations are the United States, the Soviet Union, Britain, and France. Among the minor exporters are West Germany, Czechoslovakia, Italy, China, and Israel. Table 28 shows imports of military jet aircraft, and Table 29 presents information on the sources of major weapons maintained in the developing countries. It goes as a matter of course that, within alliances, the less developed members import weapons from the more developed ones. Thus, Turkey and South Korea receive their weapons from the United States while North Vietnam and North Korea depend on the major Communist states. The major powers have also concluded numerous military aid agreements with less developed countries. These agreements not only involve the grant or usually, sale of weapons, but also concern military assistance in the form of advice and training.

Because of this copious international flow of weapons, the less developed countries are able to afford types of armament which they are unable to produce; and the vast economically underdeveloped parts of the world are full of arms manufactured in the much smaller developed parts. It is not surprising that the Kashmir war between India and Pakistan was fought with a great variety of foreign arms on both sides. However, a state without the potential to produce sophisticated weapons tends to suffer also from a low ability for employing and maintaining them effectively. This handicap can be overcome by dint of the most rigorous training and discipline; but this is the harder to do, the less the degree of industrial development, and the less the skill to work complex machinery diffused through the population. The Arab-Israeli war furnishes a telling example. Israel is not, of course, an economically underdeveloped state. Through prodigiously intensive training, the Israeli pilots achieved a remarkable mastery over the French jet aircraft they flew. The Egyptians, on the other hand, though they had received excellent military equipment from the Soviet Union, were unable to attain the levels of specialized training to use it efficiently.[108] Similarly, during the war between India and Pakistan, both sides experienced great difficulties in employing foreign tanks and other advanced military gear.[109] Nonetheless, the ability to import technologically advanced weaponry compensates considerably for that lack of industrial and technological military potential which is typical of the economically underdeveloped states.

Special Situations

During the initial phase of the Korean War, the North Korean forces gave a good account of themselves against the South Korean and American troops. The North Vietnamese regulars were far from a pushover for the American Marines in South Vietnam. The Algerian liberation army fought for years against the French and denied them a military victory. These are recent instances of special circumstances permitting economically underdeveloped and small countries, or territorial organizations typical of such countries, to put impressive military strength against larger and far more developed states. These events demonstrate that, as we have pointed out repeatedly, the significance of any one component of military strength is to a considerable extent situational. The events just referred to clearly imply that the importance of even gross differences in national economic and technological potential can diminish greatly or disappear altogether when compensating circumstances have a powerful impact. The most important such circumstances are the following eight.

First, the economically superior power operates at a far distance and thus bears the costs of voluminous resources being absorbed in the logistical task. Second, because of distance, and the need to organize the logistical operation, it takes the superior power appreciable time before it can deploy large forces far from the home base. Third, the superior state may have only small ready forces, or more likely, it may have the bulk of its resources already invested in other and perhaps more important military tasks. Fourth, the side whose material resources are grossly inferior receives large military

[108]General Beaufre, "Une guerre classique moderne," *Stratégie* (Paris, Institut Français d'Etudes Strategiques), No. 13 (1967), p. 22.
[109]*Cf.* Leo Heiman, "Lessons from the War in Kashmir," *Military Review*, XLVI (February 1966), pp. 22–29.

supplies from another superior power, and has the political and administrative capabilities to put this imported military technology to efficient use. Fifth, the theater of war has difficult natural features and poor means of transportation, and is therefore hard to penetrate and control by the highly mechanized and supply-burdened forces of the industrial state. Sixth, the superior power may be intervening in a revolutionary situation, encountering irregular warfare by forces which, though small and modestly equipped, enjoy decisive support by the local population, and thus benefit from the advantages of superior intelligence, mobility, and concealment. Seventh, political considerations, reflecting adverse attitudes and opinion at home and abroad, restrain the superior power from resorting to technically very effective methods and means of warfare. Eighth, the military forces of the industrially superior state may be inferior in generalship and troop morale. Especially when several of these conditions coincide, the military forces and potential of superior powers may be prevented from becoming effective, or at least from achieving full effectiveness.

Scale of Resources

As happens between highly industrialized countries, among the economically less developed states also, the larger or more populous tend to enjoy advantages of scale over the smaller states. Of two countries with an equally small manufacturing output, or an equally small number of scientists and engineers per capita, the one with more than a hundred million people obviously has far larger resources in absolute volume than one of only a few million inhabitants. Therefore, if the government of a very populous state is determined and able to devote a large proportion of the relevant resources to the military sector, and commands the administrative skills to exploit them efficiently, it can afford a substantial level of military production. These possibilities will be discussed briefly with reference to Mainland China and India, two economically underdeveloped states which have considerable and growing claims to military power.

Because these two large states with huge populations are no more highly developed than most less developed countries, their cases demonstrate that the acquisition of an indigenous military technology is determined less by relative wealth or poverty in per capita terms than by the absolute volume of relevant resources, and by their aggregate military expenditures. In the late 1960's China and India maintained armed forces which were numerically the third and fourth largest in the world—immediately following the Soviet Union and the United States; their defense expenditures exceed $500 million a year and their aggregate GNP's and industrial outputs rank them among the ten leading states in the world.[110] They have developed a military

[110]K. Subrahmanyam, "Defense Preparations in India and China," *Bulletin of Atomic Scientist,* May 1968, p. 28.

production base which substantially exceeds that of such other countries as Brazil, Argentina, Turkey, the United Arab Republic, Pakistan and Indonesia.

India

India has a population of 483 million (1965) which is growing at a rapid 2.3 percent a year (1958–1965). Her GNP of $49.2 billion in 1965 (converted at official exchange rates) which was only half of Japan's ($98 billion) and France's ($93 billion), but not very far behind Mainland China's estimated at $76.0 billion (which may be an overestimate), dwarfed that of countries such as Burma ($1.8 billion), and outclassed even that of Pakistan ($11.0 billion) and Indonesia ($10.5 billion). India is still decidedly underdeveloped economically. Her GNP per capita of $100 falls substantially short of those of Malaysia ($296) and Turkey ($261). It is even below Bolivia's $145,[111] but just about equal Mainland China's. Yet her GNP rose by 70 percent from 1951 to 1966, and her per capita income by 20 percent despite a population growth of 153 million.[112]

India has plenty of natural resources and, though a very high proportion of her labor force is engaged in the primary industries, she has sizeable manufacturing industries. While her total national product increased by 71 percent from 1958 to 1965, her output of electric power and of her metal-working industries rose by 156 and 153 percent respectively.[113] In 1965, she produced 6.4 million tons of steel and nearly 73,000 motor vehicles.[114] India has clearly developed a respectable infrastructure for further industrial expansion. Now that a combination of heightened government attention, and encouraging price policy, large investments in irrigation and fertilizer, and above all the influx of new foreign technology in the form of superior strains of wheat and rice, seem to have induced what may turn out to be a true breakthrough in agricultural development,[115] she has laid the groundwork for substantial industrial growth, particularly if critical foreign aid continues to be received. India may, of course, be set back periodically by a bad crop year, her foreign exchange position remains extremely tight and vulnerable, and her continued population growth acts as a drain on resources; but her overall economic prospects look at this time very good over the longer run.

With around one million men under arms (1965), India maintains

[111]All GNP data from U.S. Arms Control and Disarmament Agency, *World-Wide Military Expenditures and Related Data*, pp. 8–10.
[112]K. Subrahmanyam, *The Asian Balance of Power in the Seventies: An Indian View* (New Delhi: The Institute for Defence Studies and Analyses, 1968), p. 7.
[113]United Nations, *Statistical Yearbook 1966*, p. 157.
[114]*Ibid.*, pp. 302, 313.
[115]*Cf.* Max F. Millikan, "India in Transition, Economic Development, Performance and Prospects," *Foreign Affairs*, XLVI, April 1968, pp. 531–547; Lester R. Brown, "The Agricultural Revolution in Asia," *Foreign Affairs*, XLVI, July 1968, pp. 688–698.

larger armed forces than all other states except the U.S.S.R., the
United States, and Mainland China. France and Britain, the next
ranking countries in these terms, have military forces only about half
as large as India's. After gaining independence, India did not feel
exposed to acute military threats and, pursuing a foreign policy of
nonalignment *vis-à-vis* the emerging east-west conflict, her governments did not, until 1962, emphasize the development of military
strength, but rather gave priority to general economic development.
For the large bulk of her armaments, India relied on external sources
of supply. Thus in 1950, foreign sources (mainly Britain) accounted
for about 90 percent of her military equipment and supplies.[116] Even
from 1947 to 1962, however, Indian governments were concerned
with starting an indigenous base for weapons production and weapons development. In fact, in the late 1950's and early 1960's, the
Indian government became so eager to build a national armaments
base that many plans and projects went awry because they ignored the
severely limited, and only slowly growing, industrial and technological potential of the country. By 1962, on the eve of the border
war with China, her ordnance establishment comprised 22 factories
producing small arms and ammunition, artillery, and some jeeps and
trucks. Her aircraft industry had designed and was developing some
jet aircraft, her shipyards were turning out patrol vessels and laying
plans for building minesweepers and destroyers, and her military R
and D organization had grown to 25 research laboratories and technical establishments. India was nevertheless far from self-sufficient in
defense production. Most sophisticated conventional arms were imported or produced on license with foreign technical assistance. Her
industrial base was still relatively thin and fragmentary and, despite
persistent efforts by the Defense Science Organization, she remained
badly deficient in the supply of scientific researchers, first-rate design
engineers, and other technical personnel.

   The war with China in 1962 acted as a tremendous shock on the
Indian government and public. Since then, Indians have displayed
keen anxieties over military threats from China, and from Pakistan
acting in tandem with China. President Radhakrishnan declared in
February 1963: "The greater our economic and defense potential, the
less will be the danger from across our boarders . . . . From now on,
defense and development must be regarded as integral and related
parts of the national economic plan."[117] Shortly after the war, the
government announced a plan envisaging the doubling of the army to
825,000 men and an airforce expanded to 45 squadrons, equipped
with modern planes and other arms.[118] From 2.97 million rupees in

---

[116]Lorne J. Kavic, *India's Quest for Security, Defense Policies 1947–1965* (Berkeley,
University of California Press, 1967). For an excellent historical account of India's
defense policies, see chapters 8 and 11. Most of the information used in the following
paragraphs is based on this analysis.
[117]Quoted, *ibid.*, p. 192.
[118]*Ibid.*

1960, the Indian defense budget rose steeply to 5.21 million in 1962,[119] and 9.7 million in 1967–68,[120] representing about 3.5 percent of GNP. The plan also specified a sharp expansion of military production facilities and of military R and D. The investment in defense industry has been large and is continuing, with much of the impact still to come. This rapid and large expansion of its armed forces practically compelled India to broaden and deepen its military production base, since to equip so huge a force by imports would have generated a prohibitive balance of payments problem. Some Indian weapons have replaced foreign models (*e.g.*, the Ishapore semi-automatic rifle, a pack howitzer, some Indian designed tanks and aircraft). And a substantially larger proportion of weapons continues to be produced under foreign license from various countries rather than directly purchased abroad. The expansion of such production communicates increasing technical knowhow. It amounts to a vast industrial learning process.

Still, in 1969 India's military-technological dependence on the more advanced countries remains overwhelming, and her reliance on imports of some sophisticated weapons and components is still vital. Although improving, India's base for military R and D continues to be weak; and it is from this capability that her independence from foreign technology must be derived eventually. The question is whether the established trend foreshadows substantial independence in ten or fifteen years. According to one highly knowledgeable Indian, the country should be able to achieve this for all but the tech-nologically most sophisticated and expensive weapons systems.[121] Much of the capacity for manufacturing conventional armaments—guns, trucks, jeeps, tanks, ammunition, some simpler types of ships and aircraft, and of such operating supplies as fuel, clothing, and food—is built up in any large country as part of the normal indus-trialization process, even though higher standards of quality control make somewhat greater demands on the metallurgical, engineering, chemical and electronic industries than is exerted by ordinary com-mercial considerations. Military research and development costs can be avoided by license agreements with major industrial nations, or minimized by imitating their technology. Whether a developing country decides to import or itself produce a military item will be governed in part by economic considerations, that is, by the question of which is the cheaper way in terms of productive resources, and also in view of scarce foreign-exchange supplies, and the disposition of arms-exporting countries to extend credits or grants. As pointed out in the following section, some non-economic considerations will also influence these decisions.

[119]*Ibid.*, Appendix I.
[120]Subrahmanyam, *The Asian Balance of Power*, p. 8.
[121]Subrahmanyam, "Defense Preparations in India and China," *Bulletin of Atomic Scientists*, p. 28.

There is however, a profound difference between the relatively simple armaments and military supplies we have been discussing and the technologically very advanced military systems such as sophisticated aerospace equipment, ballistic missiles, nuclear weapons, submarines, and complex electronic systems. Their production, not to speak of their design, demands far more high-level skills and other high-cost and scarce resources; and, since these sophisticated weapon systems integrate a number of sophisticated sub-systems (e.g., propulsion and electronics), their production requires that industrial development has reached a commensurately high level in a number of fields such as rare metal alloys, machine tools, and instrumentation.[122] In order to enter these fields of advanced technology simultaneously and successfully, India need not wait until her industrialization attains the level of western Europe. In part, the development of this kind of military industrial R and D potential is a matter of the public determination to foster it, perhaps ruthlessly, at the expense of promoting other areas of development. But India must acquire larger and more sophisticated capabilities than she possesses at this time.

Currently the most interesting question is whether India, perceiving itself to be menaced by China's development of nuclear armament, will feel compelled to enter this field of military technology, and whether it could do so with sufficient prospects of achievement. This requires definitely a sophisticated technology. However, the development of nuclear energy for civilian purposes, and the worldwide diffusion of relevant scientific and technological knowledge, have inevitably provided an increasing number of countries with capabilities essential to the development and manufacture of nuclear bombs. One of these capabilities is knowhow, the other plutonium, which is a byproduct of nuclear energy production and is suitable for the making of fission bombs. The production of fission bombs requires the separation of uranium 235 from natural uranium, and this is a technically intricate and extremely expensive process (which the Chinese seem to have consummated). Certainly, the manufacture of crude fission explosives of the kind dropped by the U.S. on Hiroshima during World War II has become so easy and cheap that dozens of nations are credited with the necessary resources at this time. Requirements of highly sophisticated technology and costs mount steeply if the object is to design and test weapons of high explosive yield which are sufficiently miniaturized to fit into the bomb bay of a bomber or the nose cone of a missile; and the production of specialized, reliable, and effective delivery vehicles, whether aircraft or rockets, is likewise exacting. An expert committee of the United Nations estimated recently that a modest nuclear capability, represented by a force of from thirty to fifty jet bombers,

[122]Cf. ibid.

together with fifty medium-range missiles of 3,000 kilometer range in soft emplacements, and 100 plutonium warheads, would cost perhaps no more than $1,700 million, to be spent over a number of years.[123] However, this estimate may grossly understate the costs. The French program, though much more ambitious since it contemplates the development of fission bombs and of a Polaris type submarine as well as land-based ballistic missiles, was meant to cost $5.7 billion but is now widely expected to cost as much as $10.0 billion. Since China has developed a fusion bomb and is reported to be developing medium-range ballistic missiles, there is a serious question of whether the modest program described in the U.N. report would serve Indian strategic needs.

India is generally credited with the potential for the development of atomic (fission)bombs and, less surely, nuclear (fusion) explosives. Her Atomic Energy Commission—now with a personnel of 8,600—was established in 1948, and her first reactor went into operation in 1956. She has now three experimental reactors in operation and several power reactors under construction. In this development, India was greatly assisted by Canada, Britain, and the United States. Some Indian officials have asserted that their country could make a crude fission bomb in eighteen months at a cost of $10 to $20 million, while American specialists believe that three years and an expenditure of $50 million is a more realistic estimate.[124] However, it is doubtful that India would gain much deterrence power *vis-a-vis* China from the mere explosion of a crude fission device. According to another, more cautious, Indian estimate, India's requirements for independent deterrence would imply a development program the dimension of France's, including fission weapons and a delivery system reasonably invulnerable to a surprise first strike. To this would have to be added a comprehensive radar warning system and an efficient command-and-control network. And, unlike France, India is not disposed to reduce her conventional forces in order to develop a strategic nuclear capability. On this basis, a suitable program for India would cost $10–$15 billion.[125] Spread over ten years, this would not be beyond India's capacity, if her government were able and willing to raise defense outlays from 3 to 5 or 6 percent of a presumably growing GNP, and she might develop or import the necessary knowhow and purchase some scarce components abroad. But clearly, the task would be gigantic viewed against her present economic and technological capacity.

[123]*Cf.* United Nations, *Effects of the Possible Use of Nuclear Weapons and the Security and Economic Implications for States of the Acquisition and Further Development of these Weapons* (New York, 1968), pp. 25–27.
[124]*The New York Times*, Sept. 26, 1966, p. 1.
[125]*Cf. A Strategy for India for a Credible Posture Against a Nuclear Adversary* (New Delhi, Institute for Defence Studies and Analyses, 1968), pp. 6–8.

Caution in the use of statistical information is particularly justified in the case of the People's Republic of China. Virtually none of the data cited in this section are above strong suspicion. They are nevertheless interesting for the purpose at hand which is served by indications of large orders of magnitude.

China's people, estimated at about 700 million in 1965,[126] represent roughly one fifth of the world population. Its GNP per capita, estimated variously at $75 to $100, is within the range of the world's lowest outside Saharan Africa. (Japan's was six to seven times larger in 1965.) The total GNP in 1965 nonetheless was estimated at $76 billion.[127] Its annual military expenditures of an estimated $6 billion (estimated by others at about 10 percent of GNP) were exceeded only by those of the two superpowers, and compared with $5.9 billion in Britain, and $2.1 billion in India. The armed forces with 2.5 million men were the world's third largest in terms of numbers and stood well above India's one million in 1965. China's huge land mass is well endowed with natural resources. In 1965, it is thought to have produced fifteen million tons of steel (compared with France's 19.6 million and India's 6.4 million tons), and (in 1960) 58.5 billion kwh of electric energy (compared with 72.1 billion in France and 20.1 billion in India).[128] She manufactured 35,000 motor vehicles in 1966.[129]

Clearly, China is no longer a peasant country. It is an industrializing state. Actually, western countries had established considerable manufacturing plants in China's coastal cities before World War II, and Japan had done so extensively in Manchuria. To this must be added an astonishingly massive international transfer of industrial technology from the Soviet Union between 1953 and 1961. Apparently, the Soviet leadership then hoped to transform Communist China on the Stalinist model, in the shortest possible time, into a modern, industrialized, and militarily strong state capable of confronting the "imperialist" West in the Far East.[130] By means of large-scale loans and technical assistance, the Soviet Union helped in setting up well over 200 enterprises and projects, including the establishment of such new branches of industrial production as automobile, tractor, and aircraft manufacture; provided China with 21,000 sets of scientific-technological documents (including more than 1,400 blueprints for big enterprises); admitted 14,000 Chinese students for higher studies,

[126]United Nations, *Statistical Yearbook 1966*, p. 82.
[127]U.S. Arms Control and Disarmament Agency, *World-Wide Military Expenditures and Related Data*, pp. 8–10. Some put this estimate as low as $50 billion. *Cf.* Dwight H. Perkins, "The Chinese Economy and Its International Impact," *SAIS Review* (Johns Hopkins University), XII, (1968), p. 39.
[128]United Nations, *Statistical Yearbook 1966*, pp. 301, 357.
[129]Dick Wilson, "China's Economic Situation," *Bulletin of Atomic Scientists*, November 1967, p. 5.
[130]*Cf.* James S. Duncan, "The Developing Economy," *Bulletin of Atomic Scientists*, July 1966, p. 84.

and more than 38,000 apprentices for training, in the Soviet Union; and sent as many as 10,800 Soviet experts to give project assistance in China.[131]

From 1952 to 1957, the Chinese authorities were able to enforce a rate of savings and investment exceeding 20 percent of the country's income.[132] They also invested enormous efforts in increasing their nation's scientific and especially engineering manpower.[133] While Chinese GNP grew at a very respectable annual rate from 6 to 8 percent (1949–1957),[134] the government neglected agriculture and favored heavy investment in electric power, iron and steel, chemical and engineering industries, which are closely linked to national potential for conventional military power.[135] The output of its heavy industries was tripled from 1953 to 1957.[136] With the development of the Sino-Soviet rift, the U.S.S.R. began to withdraw assistance in 1960. Discarding the Soviet model for rapid industrial development by heavy forced savings, the Chinese leaders embarked on the "Great Leap Forward" (1958–1960), based on a frenzied political mobilization, which was a monumental failure in the end and cost the country several years of economic growth. The retreat from the "Great Leap" led to a moderate recovery and economic expansion in 1962–66, this time with emphasis on agricultural investment, but without downgrading the previous priority on military production.[137] "The Great Proletarian Cultural Revolution" which began to put China in turmoil in 1966 once again disrupted the economic system and slowed down Chinese economic progress.

Soviet technological aid helped the Chinese government to acquire, by 1960, an industrial capacity capable of equipping the Chinese army with conventional weapons. To be sure, despite progress, China is still deficient in meeting minimum requirements of alloy steels, machine tools, electronics, instrumentation, and heavy-duty automotive vehicles. But it is basically self-sufficient in the production of all military supplies which demand no advanced technological sophistication. Its huge army is equipped with modern infantry weapons (including mortars, recoilless rifles, light and medium artillery, and some rockets), being deficient mainly in heavy artillery, tanks and trucks, in complex rocketry, and electronic communications. The army's tactical mobility is good, but it is relatively weak in heavy firepower and strategic mobility, making it

---

[131]Subrahmanyam, "Defense Preparations in India and China," *Bulletin of Atomic Scientists*, p. 29.

[132]Alexander Eckstein, *Communist China's Economic Growth and Foreign Trade* (New York: McGraw-Hill, 1966), p. 303.

[133]Chu-Yuan Cheng, *Scientific and Engineering Manpower in Communist China, 1949–1963* (Washington, D.C.: National Science Foundation, 1965).

[134]Perkins, *op. cit.*, p. 28.

[135]Eckstein, *op. cit.*, p. 2.

[136]Perkins, *op. cit.*, p. 28.

[137]*Ibid.*, p. 31; Duncan, *op. cit.*, p. 86.

difficult for it to operate on any major scale beyond China's boundaries, excepting perhaps some peripheral areas in Korea and Southeast Asia.[138] On the other hand, China's air force, though fairly large, is obsolescent since it consists mostly of Soviet planes, and her navy is very small.[139]

Regarding conventional military strength, the Chinese government has used massive Soviet aid, its country's most basic asset—a talented, educable and industrious labor force—and a heavy rate of public savings and investment in order to achieve an impressive broadening and deepening of China's industrial base, and hence of its military economic potential. In 1966, China's heavy industrial production was about double that of Japan in the 1930's, when that country began to embark on an ambitious military policy.[140] In this respect, its development exceeds India's by a large margin. Outside the area of nuclear explosives, however, China's potential, like India's, does not extend to the manufacture of complex, high-cost weapon systems. The Chinese aircraft industry, for example, is still rather primitive. In the production of these sophisticated items, technological bottlenecks, characteristic of a nation at its stage of industrialization, are bound to be numerous, vexing and inhibiting.[141] It has little autonomy in the area of high-level technology, civilian and military, and also lacks the resources permitting the development of an impressive logistical mobility and reach.

China, however, is the only economically underdeveloped nation which has developed nuclear explosives; and this not by going the simpler plutonium way, but by constructing facilities for separating U–235. This is a technically intricate and extremely expensive process which allowed China to proceed straight to the production of thermonuclear devices. In this area of technology, China has indeed outperformed France.[142] This is a tremendous feat even though China was aided by the education of many scientists in the United States and even more in the Soviet Union, and even though until 1957 the latter helped China in other ways to establish a technological nuclear base.[143] The costs to China of developing nuclear explosives have been estimated at from $1 to $2 billion through 1966[144] and the costs of developing land-based ICBM's or submarine based ballistic missiles of the Polaris type are assumed to cost another $2 billion each.[145] Of course, estimates of real Chinese costs are not

---

[138]Cf. Samuel B. Griffith, "The Military Potential of China," in *China and the Peace of Asia,* ed. Alastair Buchan (New York: Frederick A. Praeger, 1965), pp. 73–74.
[139]*Ibid.,* pp. 75–76.
[140]Perkins, *op. cit.,* pp. 38–39.
[141]*Ibid.,* p. 40.
[142]89th U.S. Congress, Joint Committee on Atomic Energy, *Impact of Chinese Communist Nuclear Weapons Progress on United States National Security* (Washington, D.C., July 1967), p. 4.
[143]Cf. Subrahmanyam, *The Asian Balance of Power,* p. 5.
[144]Perkins, *op. cit.,* p. 40.
[145]Subrahmanyam, *The Asian Balance of Power,* p. 5.

meaningful. Besides, even if approximately correct, they would obviously not be prohibitive for a country whose government has the political authority to allocate 10 percent of the GNP to defense (the equivalent of $7 to $8 billion). The real feat for China lies not in being able to bear the overall expenditures but rather in overcoming a series of technological restraints from which one would expect an economy, such as the Chinese, to suffer.[146] At this time, the Chinese are credited with the capacity to develop and deploy over the next few years a rocket delivery system with nuclear warheads. It is unclear whether China could have developed this capacity without large-scale Soviet aid. The fact remains that, in this one area of sophisticated military technology, China is succeeding despite the drawbacks of her general industrial and technological deficiencies. Even though she does not now have the capacity to develop and build a sophisticated military aircraft, she has penetrated a vital area of advanced technology.

Conclusion

States with very large populations but a relatively low stage of industrial development clearly have the economic potential to produce considerable military strength of a conventional character, either by largely importing the necessary military technology (as was India's course) or by fostering a fairly indigenous base for all but highly complex military systems (as China did), although not without initial foreign aid on a spectacular scale. In the area of nuclear technology, China has succeeded in mastering even a sophisticated technology; and India is generally conceded to have a credible capacity to develop nuclear arms. These examples show that, once a certain threshold of industrialization has been crossed, a large absolute volume of resources is more critical to military economic potential than a high GNP per capita, or even a rapid rate of economic growth, helpful as these conditions undoubtedly are.

But their comparatively low level of industrialization limits India, and even China, to the production of *local* military power. Even a high rate of economic development would not lift this restraint for a long period of time.[147] Potential for world military power calls for a decidedly richer base in industry, research, and technology. The attainment of this level is at this time beyond the apparent development potential of virtually all underdeveloped states. The process of requisite development is not just continuous additions to economic resources but the entire transformation of the societies concerned. As the example of Japan indicates, this is possible. But it took even Japan a good long time to develop the necessary economic and technological base, and there is so far only one Japan.

[146]*Cf.* Perkins, *op. cit.,* p. 26.
[147]*Ibid.,* pp. 36–39.

International Trade and Finance

International trade has a bearing on the military potential of states since it affects both the size of the national product and the structure of productive resources. International finance affects the capacity of nations to draw, for military as well as other purposes, on the resources of other states. It also circumscribes their capability to operate militarily beyond national boundaries.

Foreign Trade and Economic Potential

Foreign trade permits states to emphasize those patterns of production for which their productive resources are comparatively most suited and to obtain through exchange those goods and services which they themselves can produce only at relatively great cost or cannot produce at all. By specialization, nations obtain a larger output from their productive capacity than they would if they had to be self-sufficient. Military potential is enhanced as GNP and GNP per capita are increased whether military equipment and supplies enter a nation's foreign trade or not. The effect is simply one of increasing productivity.

If a state is a large net exporter of military goods—as are at the present time the United States and the Soviet Union—this indicates the presence of substantial productive advantages in these fields of output over other nations. These advantages could be those of an appropriate industrial capacity, of superior R and D resources, and of scale. In any case, such trade is an index of high economic potential for military production. The resources producing a large and continuous export surplus in arms represent a reserve capacity which, in an emergency, can be switched to satisfy expanded national requirements.

On the other hand, to the extent that a state does not possess a resource base appropriate to producing military goods, it is much better off *economically*, if it obtains these abroad in peacetime, and if possible also in time of war, in exchange for export goods which it is comparatively better equipped to produce. Through trade, the country can presumably afford more military goods at a given level of expenditures, or it can secure a given volume of military supplies at a lesser outlay. As we have seen in the foregoing most economically underdeveloped states are incapable of manufacturing weapons requiring sophisticated industrial resources to produce. Without trade (or sometimes gifts), these countries would not have heavy artillery, tanks, military aircraft, and most other types of modern military equipment. Their military forces would be reduced to the kind of equipment prevalent in the pre-industrial or in the early industrial age. Only the flourishing trade in arms has made possible the worldwide proliferation of armed forces equipped with technologically advanced weapons. One characteristic of all wars since World War II—excepting the United States fighting in Korea and Vietnam—is that the vast bulk of the weapons with which they were waged were not produced by the belligerent states.

In fact, even most of the rich and highly industrialized countries lack the advantages of scale and the specialized industrial and R and D resources to keep anywhere near full pace with the military technology of the two giants. Only the United Kingdom and France in Europe have some proven capacity in jet engine design and a considerable competence in developing and manufacturing a vast range and succession of military missiles.[148] Thus all industrial countries in western Europe import a considerable, though varying amount of military equipment. From 1955 to 1967, for instance, Britain made direct purchases from the United States of the Phantom fighter, C–130 transport, Polaris missile, Dreadnought nuclear reactor, Sidewinder, Corporal and Honest John missiles, Chinook helicopter, and two heavy artillery guns. She also bought a missile in France, another type in Sweden, and a helicopter and howitzer in Italy.[149] The French list of imports is of similar extent, and those of West Germany and the other west European states are much longer.[150] Nearly all the sophisticated conventional arms in the east European countries are imported from the Soviet Union.[151] In addition, the west European states produced a large proportion of domestically manufactured armament on foreign licenses, which amounts to an import of military technology, and they produce a lesser proportion by means of joint procurement arrangements.[152] The impact of American military technology on western Europe, and of Soviet military technology on eastern Europe is overwhelming. In the mid-1960's, for example, no more than 60 percent of the 25,000 military aircraft in the hands of the European NATO powers had been built in Europe, and a high proportion of these were trainers and helicopters.[153] As we noted above in the case of India, a number of non-European countries also produce a great deal of military equipment on license. This holds especially true of Japan—which makes Nike-Hercules and Hawk missiles, helicopters, and jet fighters on license—but occurs also, though on a slight scale, excepting India, in the economically less developed countries.

Although the import of foreign arms or foreign arms technology is often a matter of sheer necessity, and is apparently more economical (usually by a large margin), a number of considerations militate against reliance on foreign arms and foreign knowhow in arms

[148]Harlow, *op. cit.,* pp. 9–10.
[149]*Ibid.,* p. 24.
[150]*Ibid.*
[151]*Cf.* The Institute for Strategic Studies, *The Military Balance 1967–1968* (London, 1967).
[152]Harlow, *op. cit.,* pp. 26–27.
[153]Buchan, *op. cit.,* p. 3.

manufacture. Dependence on foreign arms is, first of all, hurtful to national pride and frustrates desire for prestige; and these feelings get easily entangled with aspirations to international status. In the industrially most advanced countries, it is particularly participation, if not leadership, in high technology which is a matter of pride. And these feelings are often magnified by the exaggerated assumption that military R and D-produced inventions are of great, if not decisive, benefit to innovation in the civil economy, and are thus a precondition of a generally high competitive standing in industrial production. The choice of foreign suppliers frequently raises questions of political compatibility. Alliance relationships may preclude shopping for the best bargain or for top quality. While an arms-importing country might be best off by sticking to one major exporting state, since this would insure standardized equipment, political as well as financial considerations may argue otherwise. Thus, as India has done, many less developed states wish to demonstrate their political nonalignment or independence by using more than one source of supply.

Several pragmatic considerations may affect decisions on whether to produce nationally or rely on trade. First, time pressure—that is, the need to have supplies available as soon as possible, which is usually dictated by the requirement to match a potential opponent—will often argue for imports. Second, the question of weapons suitability may be critical. The western European countries may be pushed in the direction of foreign weapon design by the high weapon standards of the U.S.S.R. which has been regarded as the main security threat by the governments of these countries.[154] But India is concerned with weapons capable of performing at Himalayan altitudes which foreign suppliers may not make. Third, when the number or value of the required equipment is small, it will hardly pay to introduce domestic production; but a weak balance-of-payments position may favor domestic production in order to conserve foreign exchange (although there is also the question of whether the country concerned would not be better off if it increased its exports or reduced its dependence on imports of non-military goods). Fourth, the desire to combat unemployment in domestic manufacturing industries may argue against arms imports.

From an economic point of view, dependence on imported armaments is, of course, especially attractive when military equipment is extended as gifts, rather than as export sales. Since World War II, the United States has been virtually the only big arms supplier making a large volume of weapons and other military items available to many allies and client states on the basis of grants;[155] and even the United States has been doing so decreasingly during the 1960's. The

---

[154]*Ibid.*, p. 4.
[155]Sutton and Kemp, *op. cit.*, p. 3.

Soviet Union has normally preferred sales.[156] However, the line between sale and grant is often obscure when a sale takes place at very low prices and/or is accompanied by an extension of long-term credit at low interest rates and perhaps with an expectation, that repayment may be deferred indefinitely if the importing state suffers from a weak balance of payments. Such "soft" loans may contain a considerable grant element. To the extent that grants occur, whether formally or informally, there is, of course, always the possibility that the arms-importing country is expected to make payment in some non-financial form, *e.g.,* in terms of political allegiance. Furthermore, there is sometimes a formal *quid-pro-quo,* other than financial, in order to pay for arms imports. Thus, base-rights extended to the arms-exporting country may be the other part of the bargain. In the summer of 1968, for instance, Spain demanded about $1 billion of military aid in exchange for extending United States military bases in Spain for another five years.[157]

However, whenever governments have the option of resorting to national production or relying on foreign purchase, it is the fact that dependence on international trade is precarious for other than financial reasons which looms large in their deliberations. Especially in wartime, though unhindered trade will even then benefit belligerent nations, trade is notoriously subject to interruption. War cuts trade with enemy states and the areas they control; blockade and counter-blockade may obstruct traffic with neutral areas; and a dearth of shipping may further limit the ability to meet urgent and swollen military requirements through international commerce. (It has been estimated that World War II interrupted about 43 percent of the volume of prewar trade.[158])

Even in the absence of direct military interference with foreign trade, dependence on external sources of armaments often spells a degree of political dependence on the exporting country, and this can turn out to be extremely precarious in time of international crises or conflict. For example, Cuba was primarily stocked with American arms when Castro's revolution led to a rupture of trade with the United States, thus removing her ability to secure ammunition, spare parts, and replacements. Cuba succeeded in buying Belgian small arms immediately, and later shifted to armaments from the Soviet Union and Czechoslovakia. When military conflict broke out in the Horn of Africa, the United States and the Soviet Union, the major arms suppliers of Ethiopia and Somalia respectively, joined in applying strong pressure in order to halt the fighting. Following the Kashmir war between India and Pakistan in 1965, the United States, a major arms supplier to both, suspended shipments for a time. Im-

---

[156]*Ibid.,* p. 2.
[157]*The New York Times,* August 11, 1968, p. 1.
[158]Knorr, *The War Potential of Nations,* p. 202.

mediately after the brief Israeli-Arab war in the summer of 1967, France declared an arms embargo which greatly hampered Israel with her dependence on the French Mirage jet fighter. When a right-wing military junta overthrew the Greek government in 1967, the United States withheld shipments of heavy arms even though Greece was a NATO ally. In all these instances, and many more, dependence on foreign armament clearly curtailed the importing state's freedom of action.

Indisputably, reliance on foreign arms is a risk and hence a source of weakness which most states will prefer to avoid or minimize, and which, if there is a real option to turn to domestic production, will be balanced against the economic advantage of international trade. Reliance on supplies from allies may reduce this vulnerability, but it does not dependably remove it. It clearly depends upon the circumstances of each case whether, and to what extent, such reliance boosts or diminishes a state's military potential. But since the configuration of these circumstances is hard or impossible to predict for the long run, the element of risk is substantial in practically all cases, and national military potential must be discounted correspondingly.

For this reason, it is not surprising to see states—notably Mainland China and India—foster their non-military production and R and D as soon as they can, and to an extent which sensitivity to high costs should make unpalatable. It also follows from this point of view, that dependence upon foreign technology only is far less precarious than dependence on the foreign purchase of finished equipment. If a country has the industrial capacity to produce on foreign license, and thus exploit foreign knowhow, an uninterrupted supply of spare parts, replacements, and additions is under its own control, although even this may be strictly speaking less economic or take more time than arms imports would. As mentioned earlier, such licensing agreements have enabled India, Japan, and numerous other countries to benefit from foreign military R and D innovations for their own arms production. This is not, however, an alternative to national R and D in some critical areas of military technology where foreign licenses are unavailable for international transfer. Nuclear arms are an example and militarily the most significant case of this kind of limitation.

International Finance

The ability of a state to run a substantial import surplus—either on the strength of large reserves of international purchasing power, or of a high foreign credit standing—permits it, at least for a time, to develop larger or better equipped armed forces than it could on its own. To the extent of the imports surplus, it draws on the productive resources of other countries either directly, by importing arms or armament-related goods, or indirectly, by importing more non-military merchandise (or by exporting less), thereby releasing its own production factors to the military sector. Such an ability to run an import surplus can be regarded as part of a state's economic military potential. Of course, a country may also be able to add unrequited imports because allies or other friendly states extend gifts or credits for essentially political reasons. In that case, no *economic* potential is involved. In fact, the ability of a nation to afford unrequited imports in support of an increased military effort originates usually in foreign political support. For this reason, a state which normally turns out a substantial export surplus and, as a result, accumulates large reserves of hard foreign currencies and large holdings of foreign investments in countries with easily convertible currencies, possesses a great asset in the event it faces the necessity of a major military effort. To gain an accession of foreign resources by a process of net foreign disinvestment can be a great advantage in time of war. During World War II, Britain's external disinvestment came to $4.2 billion.[159]

The maintenance and use of military forces beyond a state's boundaries will also cost foreign exchange—e.g., in payment of fuel and other supplies and services bought abroad—except to the extent that foreign countries have accepted to bear this burden. For the United States and the United Kingdom to maintain sizable forces in West Germany is costly in terms of foreign exchange although, in this case, the West German government has largely offset this currency drain by importing American and British arms, and by buying securities of these countries. Similarly, it costs foreign exchange for the United States and the Soviet Union to operate fleets in the Mediterranean and other oceans. The United States fighting in Vietnam led to sizable direct foreign-exchange outlays as well as to indirect losses of international reserves, in large part induced by an increasing federal budget deficit, which accelerated inflation, made American exports less competitive and expanded the American demand for imports.

From the viewpoint of exerting worldwide military power, the weakening of the American balance of payments, and the dollar, especially in 1967 and 1968, is an interesting case of limited capability and potential in this respect. In 1949, the United States owned gold reserves of $25.5 billion, and net monetary reserves of $22.8 billion. Its international financial strength was so enormous that it could afford the Marshall Plan for the recovery of Europe and a broadening stream of economic aid to the economically underdeveloped world, while still maintaining considerable military forces and bases all over the world. Beginning in 1958, when Europe's recovery had been completed, this strong position of external financial liquidity began to weaken. The country ran huge and persistent payments deficits for several years and, by the end of 1967, its gold hoard had shrunk to a little over $10 billion, and its net monetary

[159]*Ibid.*, p. 262.

reserve position had turned negative by several billion dollars. The inflationary pressures occasioned by the war in Vietnam finally touched off a serious crisis of confidence in the U.S. dollar. Beyond question, the United States faces the necessity of putting its financial house in order, although—since the dollar also functions as an international currency for many other states—any serious attempt to restore equilibrium to the United States balance of payments will probably have to be accompanied by a reform of the entire world monetary system.[160] To be sure, the international monetary position of the United States is basically far stronger than Britain's has been in recent years. This country has an export surplus which is normally very large—reflecting the international competitiveness of its economy. It has a gold reserve which is still rather large in relation to its foreign trade; and, until the war in Vietnam expanded, its internal monetary stability compared well with that of most industrial countries. Nevertheless, restoring equilibrium in the international financial transactions of the United States will require substantial adjustments. If its trade balance does not expand considerably, it will be unable, over the longer run, to afford large and persistent military outlays abroad on top of foreign aid, huge foreign investments by American firms, and huge expenditures made by American tourists abroad. Strong as the United States is internationally in economic and financial terms, there are definite limits to its capacity to finance military missions overseas.

Not rarely, the strain of external finance is only one factor of several inducing the retrenchment of military forces stationed abroad. The gradual withdrawal of British military forces from the Mediterranean, the Indian Ocean area and elsewhere has often been attributed to the urgings of repetitive crises which struck the pound sterling after World War II. Actually, the United Kingdom's retrenchment as a world military power was brought about by a number of conditions. One important factor, perhaps the most important, was that the progressive decolonization of her former Empire automatically reduced British military responsibilities overseas. There was the further political change that, over the past two decades, the utility of military power, particularly of the military power of western nations, engaged on behalf of various traditional objectives has been decidedly on the decline, partly because such uses have lost in international legitimacy, and partly because the rise of nationalism and the development of local military strength in the underdeveloped world, and also the strong Soviet opposition to western power plays in this world. To protect one's oil investments by dispatching a few gunboats no longer is either acceptable or effective. The age of such old-fashioned imperialism is dead.

No doubt, economic stringencies also played a big part in

[160]Cf. C. Fred Bergsten, "Taking the Monetary Initiative," Foreign Affairs, XLVI, July 1968, pp. 713–732; Robert Triffin, "Neither Gold Nor the Dollar," The New Republic, January 27, 1968, pp. 23–26.

Britain's military retreat from much of the world. Against the background of a national income growing at an exceptionally low rate, her postwar disposition to let the volume of demand from all sources exceed the volume of supply did put pressure on her balance of payments and led to several severe crises of the pound. Whenever remedial action could no longer be postponed, military outlays were as legitimate a candidate for cutbacks as any other type of national expenditures. The direct foreign-exchange costs of British forces stationed overseas were relatively too small to constitute a major source of relief. It is true, however, that when Britain, along with France and Israel, launched military operations against Egypt in 1956, it was not so much Soviet military threats which caused her to desist. The pressure which really hurt resulted from a loss of gold and dollar reserves which began in September and reached almost $280 million by November 1956. When the United States withheld financial backing, the British government decided to yield, and the Suez crisis came to an end.[161] On the other hand, when the United Kingdom followed the 1968 devaluation of her currency with abandoning its military commitments east of Suez altogether, and also cancelled the plan to buy American planes to replace her aging bomber fleet, on which her strategic detterent capability rested in large part, the prospect of foreign-exchange savings were apparently a minor consideration. These military cuts rather seemed to have served the political function of securing enough Labour-Party support for the cabinet's plan to enforce a substantial restraint on domestic consumption.[162] Foreign exchange pressures probably contributed to the progressive shrinking of Britain's military might after World War II. Yet to the extent that economic conditions pushed in this direction, they worked toward a reduction of a military role which, in the contemporary world, a nation of her size could exceed for long only by placing a higher priority on such power than the electorate was prepared to grant. In justifying the military costs, Prime Minister Wilson remarked that it "is not only at home that, these past years, we have been living beyond our means."[163] But, as one observer put it: "Economy was more the occasion than the cause . . .the will to soldier on had gone, and not just in Labour ranks."[164]

To conclude, a state's strength in international trade and finance contributes significantly to its military economic potential. Countries differ greatly in this respect. As is to be expected, the situation of the less developed states is typically one of perennial shortages of foreign exchange. For instance, at the end of the first quarter of 1967, the industrial nations held 87 percent of the world's total gold reserves of

[161]Cf. Carey B. Joynt, "John Foster Dulles and the Suez Crisis," in Statesmen and Statecraft of the Modern West: Essays in Honor of Dwight E. Lee and H. Donaldson Jordan, ed. Gerald NN. Greb (Barre, Mass., 1967), pp. 233–234.
[162]"The Washing of Hands," The Economist (London), January 20, 1968, p. 18.
[163]The New York Times, January 17, 1968, p. 14.
[164]Brian Wenham, "Britain First," The New Republic, February 3, 1968, p. 9.

$40.4 billion. India and Pakistan possessed only $243 million and $53 million respectively, while the United States had $13,184 million's worth, and England $1,677 million.[165] Within the group of industrial states, the weakened position of the United States had led to a great strengthening of the position of such European countries as West Germany, France, Italy, and Switzerland. Such comparisons are, of course, incomplete and gross. A more meaningful comparison relates all readily available means of international liquidity to each state's volume of imports. On this basis, gold and immediate foreign-exchange reserves of West Germany were enough to finance four-and-one-half months' volume of imports, compared with about five months for the United States, and one-and-a-half months' for India.

Comparative Economic Systems

The question is often raised whether the kind of economic system under which a society operates significantly affects its military potential. Partisans have extolled the "capitalist" or the "communist" system from this point of view. What type of economic order a society maintains, and how it changes that order over time, is fundamentally a *political* decision. But the decision which is made has crucial consequences for *economic* performance.

Whatever the structure of its economy, every society faces the same basic questions: What should be the quantity and composition of goods and services produced? How should productive resources be organized for the production of each commodity and service? How is the accruing output to be distributed among the population? How much of aggregate income is to be saved and invested each year? How is technological innovation to be managed?[166]

Under the pure capitalist system, these decisions are made overwhelmingly not by state authorities but, in a highly decentralized fashion, are left to the discretion of private individuals. Effective consumer demand determines the size and composition of output; based on private ownership in the means of production, the private entrepreneur determines the techniques of production, innovation and investment. Under a pure socialist system, at least as it informed the first generation of Communist leaders in the U.S.S.R., the state owns all means of production (except labor), and the state—whose authorities identify and express the popular will—make all types of economic decisions directly or indirectly. Under the pure capitalist

[165]From International Monetary Fund, *International Financial Statistics* (Washington, D.C., August 1968), p. 15.
[166]On economic systems, see Walter Eucken, *The Foundations of Economics* (Chicago: University of Chicago Press, 1951); George N. Hahn, *Economic Systems, A Comparative Analysis* (New York: Holt, Rinehart & Winston, 1951); Alfred R. Oxenfeldt, *Economic Systems in Action*, rev. ed. (New York: Holt, Rinehart & Winston, 1952); Nathaniel S. Preston, *Politics, Economics and Power* (New York, The Macmillan Company, 1967).

system, prices must be left free to fluctuate in order to bring the demand for and supply of goods and services, savings and investment into equilibrium; and special rewards are given to the entrepreneur (profit) and to the owner of capital and land (interest, rent). Under the pure Soviet-type socialist system, prices are fixed by authorities, income from ownership is eliminated and no special type of reward is held out to entrepreneurs and innovators. It is also conceivable that a socialist economic order could be constructed to combine consumer sovereignty through an appropriately free price system—with public ownership in the means of production.[167]

It is easy to see that types of economic systems could affect the military potential of nations if they had a different effect on economic growth and industrialization, the structure of productive resources, the rate and direction of technological advance, and the international financial standing of communities. But though it is likely that the basic form of economic regime impinges on the capability of national economies, the exact repercussions are obscure for two chief reasons.

First, all *actual* economic systems deviate from the pure models. This holds true of the capitalist, or free-enterprise systems, which as a group are today vastly different from the conceptual constructs that inspired Adam Smith and excited Karl Marx. To varying extents, all existing systems in the industrial countries which could be included in this category feature a substantial, though varying, admixture of public enterprise (especially Italy, France, Britain), have conferred on central government authorities varying but strong interventionary power in the economy (*e.g.,* monetary and fiscal policy, public investment, price controls), and operate "free markets" which are variously restricted by business monopolies, labor unions, etc.

On the other hand, the Communist states have always tolerated at least a marginal amount of private enterprise and free markets; and they are currently facing vexing problems of bureaucratic control, clumsy investment, output and price planning, and poor performance in important branches of their economies. In the Soviet Union, for example, the performance of agriculture, consumer-goods industries, and residential construction has always been a weakness of the economic regime. As a result, several member countries (*e.g.,* Yugoslavia, East Germany, Hungary) have initiated institutional experiments designed to decentralize economic decision-making and accord prices and consumer demand a bigger role in the allocation of productive resources.[168] It looks at present as if these reforms of their economic systems will lead to different regimes in the Communist states even though they are determined to retain the crucial feature of

---

[167]*Cf.* Oskar Lange and Fred M. Taylor, *On the Economic Theory of Socialism* (Minneapolis: University of Minnesota Press, 1938, 1952).

[168]On recent changes in the Soviet Union see: Gertrude Schroeder, "Soviet Economic 'Reforms" A Study in Contradictions," *Soviet Studies,* XX (July 1968), pp. 1–21; Michael Ellman, "Optimal Planning," *ibid.,* pp. 112–136; Alec Nove, "Russian Money Matters," *New Statesman* (London), October 20, 1967, p. 509.

overall ownership in the means of production. Thus, as the so-called free-enterprise countries have greatly expanded the economic role of central governments, the Communist countries are attempting to improve economic performance by decentralizing economic decision-making. Not surprisingly, some observers predict a convergent trend in the economic systems of these two groups of industrial nations.[169]

The economically less developed countries employ various widely differing and frequently changing, mixtures of free-enterprise, socialist and traditional (*i.e.,* pre-modern) patterns of economic decision-making. Some are communist (*e.g.,* China, North Vietnam); many others lean, at least at present, strongly toward a strong socialist or state-capitalist component (*e.g.,* Algeria, the United Arab Republic, Burma); while others give considerable room to private enterprise (*e.g.,* Lebanon, the Philippines, Brazil). At any rate, their national economic regimes look chaotic or kaleidoscopic when approached from the viewpoint of pure, basic systems. Thus, the bewilderingly mixed character of actual economic systems makes it difficult to deduce performance or capability consequences from the abstract properties which characterize the pure models.

Second, any effect which the structure of economic systems might exert on national economic capabilities are hard to separate, if not inseparable, from the impact of other conditions. For example, if the Soviet productivity of labor and capital investments is, though gaining over time, low in comparison with that of the United States or West Germany,[170] we do not know whether this results from differences in economic systems or in the stage of economic development, or some other factors. Moreover, to the extent that central governments occupy a more or less strategic position in the direction of all national economies everywhere, performance and capability reflect differences in administrative competence and in the *political* power of governments as well as differences of economic order. Surely, if communist systems display a high rate of forced savings and investments, it results from the political power of governments—which might change— rather than from the nature of their economic system of decision-making. Innovation, which plays a key role in economic progress everywhere is, according to our previous analysis, a many-rooted phenomenon, depending especially on public education, government support, and social consensus on the net value of technological advancement. Cultural factors, shaping labor mobility, work discipline, and many other conditions of consequence to national economic capacity, vary greatly among states even though industrialization, in turn, has similar effects on cultural and social patterns wherever it

[169]*Cf.* H. Linnemann, J.P. Pronk and J. Tinbergen, "Convergence of Economic Systems in East and West," in *Disarmament and World Economic Interdependence,* ed. Emile Benoit (New York: Columbia University Press, 1967), pp. 246–260.
[170]*Cf.* 90th U.S. Congress, Joint Economic Committee, *Soviet Economic Performance: 1966–67,* p. 14.

occurs. If one tries to describe Britain, the United States, and Japan all simply as "capitalist" systems, one refers to a formal abstraction which, at the present state of our knowledge at any rate, seems to catch very little of what makes national economies pulse and produce, flourish and decay.

In any case, vastly different as they still are in terms of their economic systems, both the Soviet Union and the United States have a huge economic military potential, just as Czechoslovakia and Australia have a far smaller one. The factors of scale and the stage of industrial and technological development are highly determinative of such potential. It seems correct to infer that the impact of formal arrangements for economic decision-making is relatively small. It may be pointed out that the "capitalist" system is more efficient in satisfying consumers' preferences, and the "socialist" system more efficient in providing public goods and services, of which defense is of course one. But the performance of states with different types of economic systems in World War II fails to sustain the obvious conclusion. Neither do the performances of the defense sector of the American and Soviet economies since World War II. The sensible conclusion is that a study of the military potential of states is guided best by focusing on actual national economies rather than on formal system identification.

4 Administrative Capabilities

Once the authorities have decided how much of national productive capacity and, to some extent, what kinds of productive factors are to be employed in the military sector of society, the amount and kind of military strength which will be generated depends importantly on the quality of administrative decisions within that sector. Whether a particular volume of resources produces more or less military strength, or military strength of the right or wrong kind, with reference to future contingencies, is in large part a function of administrative competence. Administrative skill would not, of course, matter if it were approximately equal in all states with important military relationships. In that case, the other components of strength would prevail. But though, as we shall see, it is virtually impossible to measure, and thus rigorously to compare, the administrative capacity of nations, there is no more reason to assume an internationally even distribution of this resource than of any other type of resource impinging on military potential. Indeed, the annals of history are full of instances revealing the importance, often decisive, of this factor in the military fate of states.

History dwells not only on famous generals and prodigious warriors but also on leaders who were exceptionally efficient and innovative in the *organization* of military effort—such men as Richelieu, Le Tellier, Louvoix, and Vauban, who were instrumental in elevating France to great military power in the seventeenth century,[1]

---

[1]*Cf.* Henry Guerlac, "Vauban: The Impact of Science on War," in *Makers of Modern Strategy*, ed. Edward M. Earle (Princeton: Princeton University Press, 1943), Ch. II.

and Carnet who, as minister of war, did so during the time of the French Revolution. It was largely superb organization of available resources which permitted Sweden, with a small population, to become a major European power under Gustavus Adolphus;[2] and it was the administrative skill of Frederick William I, and the organizational genius of Frederick the Great which transformed Prussia into a military power able to assert itself against the combined strength of Russia, Austria, and France in the eighteenth century. Prussia—which was vastly inferior to these big powers in population and economic resources—so succeeded partly by luck, but mainly because it made militarily the most of its relatively meager resources.[3] When the subsequent decay of the Prussian army led to the defeats by Napoleon in 1806, it was the administrative reforms undertaken by Stein, Hardenberg, and Yorck[4] which once more forged the Prussian army into a mighty fighting force. These reforms had political purpose and effect, evoking a surge of popular commitment to Prussia's war effort against Napoleon, but they also adapted the organization of military strength, and even military tactics, to the new spirit. Subsequently, the Prussian army developed in its famed general staff a splendid administrative instrument for organizing war. Prussia's victory in the Franco-Prussian War of 1870–71 is attributed in large part to her superior organization of mobilization and deployment, which was directed by the general staff.[5]

In recent history perhaps no better examples of the decisiveness of administrative failure are furnished than by the record of France in World Wars I and II. Prior to World War I, French military leaders, with Foch perhaps outstanding, based military preparations single-mindedly and inflexibly on the exploitation of French "élan" and "will" to fire an exclusively offensive strategy and tactics.[6] They did so at a time when military technology—especially the machine gun—was strongly favoring the defensive. Following World War I, French leadership subscribed with equal tenacity to a strictly defensive doctrine[7]—epitomized in the celebrated Maginot Line—while the Germans with great skill organized a fighting machine, built on the mobility of tank and aircraft, and the tactics of *blitzkreig,* which swiftly crushed the French defenses in 1940. These examples could be easily multiplied. They all tell the same story, namely, that

---

[2]*Cf.* E. V. Wedgwood, *The Thirty Years War* (New York: Doubleday & Co., 1961), pp. 261–263.

[3]Walter Dorn, *Competition for Empire, 1740–1763* (New York: Harper & Row, 1940), pp. 90 ff.; Peter Paret, *Yorck and the Era of Prussian Reform, 1807–1815* (Princeton: Princeton University Press, 1966), Ch. II on the "Frederician Age."

[4]Paret, *op. cit.,* Ch. IV–VI.

[5]Michael Howard, *The Franco-Prussian War* (New York: The Macmillan Company, 1961), pp. 18–29.

[6]Stefan T. Possony and Etienne Mantoux, "Du Picq and Foch: The French School," in Earle, *Makers of Modern Strategy,* Ch. 9.

[7]*Cf.* André Beaufre, *1940: The Fall of France* (London: Cassell, 1967).
Proceedings, May 1968, p. 293.

administrative skill in shaping military strength, and hence that administrative potential, is an important constituent of a nation's military potential.

Military Decision-Making

In the modern age, what we call here administrative competence is required for making and implementing a vast array of decisions which, together with resources, determine a state's putative military power. Thus, there is the distribution of military manpower and equipment over the different types of forces, possibly nuclear and non-nuclear, operating on land, in and on the sea, in the air and in outer space. Which are the most efficient combinations of numbers of men, length of training, and volume of equipment? What should be the size and composition of military stocks? How should military officers be educated? How many and which military bases should be maintained abroad? What should be the ratio of expenditures between the procurement of designed weapons and the development of improved or entirely new arms? On what areas of new technology should military R and D place its main bets? What proportion of resources should be devoted to mobility, to strategic and tactical versatility, to military intelligence, to military contingency planning, to military communications systems?

The people who make and implement such decisions occupy a variety of roles. The precise structure of these roles varies from state to state. Because of their professional expertise, the military obviously take part in making decisions in the military sector. But the extent to which decisions are assumed by, or delegated to them, depends on purpose, scope, and effectiveness of civilian control over the military. Such control is small, if not negligible or completely absent, in states, where the military form or dominate the government. In the past, states with democratic forms of government often left most decisions on strategy, military doctrine, force structure, and equipment to the military, reserving only control over the aggregate budget. At the present time, civilian control is extensive in all industrialized countries, and also in all those which occupy the higher ranks of military power.

In these states, the relevant "administrative" structure may be more or less centralized or pluralist, but it is very complex. In the United States, for instance, the military services, the Joint Chiefs of Staff, the Department of Defense with its complicated structure of civilian subdepartments and agencies, and the President and his office, represent the central core of the structure. But the Department of State, the Arms Control and Disarmament Agency, the Bureau of the Budget, the Atomic Energy Commission, and—on the legislative side—several Congressional committees and subcommittees are more or less involved in various decisions. In the Soviet Union, the

Presidium, the Central Committee of the Communist Party, several ministries, GOSPLAN (the state agency for overall economic planning), and the military share in making the important decisions. The other industrial countries and also many less developed states—such as India and China—maintain a similarly complex administrative apparatus. The professional competence of those involved in the administration of the military effort covers a considerable spectrum, including the skills of the policitian, the professional military, the civil servant, the natural scientist, engineer, economist, and statistician.

All major military decisions—which, in their implementation, require decisions about scores, if not hundreds, of problems—are made within a framework of assumptions concerning objectives, strategies, contingencies, and available resources. To formulate this set of assumptions, and revise it in the light of continuously changing circumstances, is in fact the key administrative task. It necessarily transcends the competence of military leaders and defense ministries. Setting out and adapting the guiding framework involves the top leadership of the state and government agencies concerned with foreign, economic, and financial affairs.

The tasks to be performed, and the skills needed for their performance, are so many and so interrelated that they tend to involve nearly the whole range of governmental activities. The following discussion, however, concentrates on administrative tasks and skills more immediately engaged in shaping military capabilities. This restriction is not adopted because the neglected tasks are unimportant. Clearly, skill in formulating and conducting foreign policy centrally affects the demands made on a state's military forces. As pointed out in Chapter I, the use of these forces by way of threats or war can be undertaken with more or less skill in international bargaining encounters. The ability to manage financially an armament effort or a limited war rests on the administrative competence of authorities in charge of monetary and fiscal policy. But the vast range of administrative tasks and skills involved in these kinds of activities is beyond the scope of this study, which is limited to the main tasks usually entrusted to departments of defense and the top echelons of the military.

The scope of the present study is restricted further in that it does not deal with the classical problems of bureaucratic administration which follow from the differential allocation of power and authority in these entities. These problems—such as the balance between centralization and decentralization, or the fact that members of such organizations tend to deviate from the behavior they are meant to display through the chain of command—pertain to the management of the military sector of society. No doubt, states which do better than others in solving these perennial problems tend to have a greater administrative potential for generating and utilizing military force. But, aside from the general nature of these problems of bureaucracy, the absence of a clearly stated theory of such organizations[8] prevents meaningful comparison. If there were a theory which identified various administrative inputs and outputs and clarified their inter-relationships, then it would be possible to seek appropriate indicators of general administrative capability and undertake international comparisons.

Principal Difficulties and Administrative Resources

The making of administrative decisions *within* the military sector is dominated by four major difficulties. The first two may be regarded as basically technical. Their nature is indicated by the criteria which United States Secretary of Defense McNamara laid down for reviewing the proposals submitted by the individual military services:

1. The mission to be accomplished.
2. The cost-effectiveness relationships among the various alternative means of performing the mission and,
3. The latest intelligence data on the capabilities of the Soviet Union and its satellites.[9]

The operative criteria are the necessity to meet the capabilities of potential opponents, and the need to economize resources.

The first difficulty then, is that decisions on military forces must be made with reference to *future* contingencies which have necessarily uncertain identity and properties. These uncertainties are obvious as long as a state is preparing for possible future conflicts. But even when a state is already engaged in war, its leaders must reckon with the possibility that the conflict will grow in scope or intensity, that other conflicts might break out, or that other more or less predictable circumstances might arise which affect the military equations. Of course, the authorities will structure their military effort mainly so as to be able to match or out-match a particular opponent or opponents whose identity is clear. However, aside from the fact that the capabilities of assumed opponents may be shrouded in some uncertainty, and will in any case change over time, the outcome of wars or of crises in which threats are employed is always subject to various other circumstances (*e.g.,* alliance relationships on both sides) that are hard or impossible to predict. Coping with these uncertainties is certainly a burden on administrative capacity.

Second, all these decisions must be made with reference to the perennial condition that aggregate resources are scarce in relation to their many possible uses. No matter how wealthy a state, its government knows limits—economic and political—to what it can afford in the militiary or any other sector. The necessity to economize poses

---

[8]William A. Niskanen, "Nonmarket Decision Making, the Peculiar Economics of Bureaucracy," *American Economic Review,* Papers and Proceedings, May 1968, p. 293.
[9]Secretary of Defense Robert F. McNamara testimony before the House Committee on Armed Services, 1962, quoted in Baldwin, *The Structure of the Defense Market,* p. 86.

endless choices which must be exercised. Is it better to build more aircraft carriers or more submarines? Should the navy have fewer nuclear-powered ships, which are more expensive, or more conventionally-fueled vessels? Is it more important to develop a new bombing plane or a new intercontinental ballistic missile? Is it wiser to expand amphibious landing capabilities or air mobility by means of helicopters? And so on. From this point of view, the best allocative performance will either generate more amilitary strength from a given input of resources or insure a given military effort at lesser costs in terms of other social goals.

Actually, criteria of force or weapon performance (quality) and of the time it takes to develop or procure a military force or weapon often complicate considerations of "cost effectiveness."[10] Pursuit of the three values inherent in these criteria is frequently competitive, that is to say, higher performance may mean more costs and more time for development or production; a "crash" program to cut the time required may entail higher costs or lower quality. This poses the problem of discovering trade-offs among the three values, which are satisfactory if not optimal. However, unless quality of performance or time pressure are brought in for extraneous reasons—"only the best is good enough"—then their introduction into costing reflects simply the first difficulty. The importance of time and quality is usually fixed by the capabilities of political military adversaries.

If these two were the only difficulties inherent in directing the transformation of military potential into actual military strength, the problems would be formidable but essentially technical; that is, in principle capable of resolution by administrative skill. To the extent that the formulation and implementation of military policy can be, and is, treated as a technical problem, rational procedure prescribes that, once national goals and objectives are clarified, different means toward goal achievement are identified, compared in their social costs and consequences (including the probability with which other costs and consequences should be expected to arise); and that the course of action ranking highest in net goal achievement be chosen. Viewed as a technical problem, this is rational procedure regardless of whether the question at issue concerns the development of a new infantry rifle, the strengthening of the navy relative to the army, the expansion of the military budget, or a decision to apply military force internationally. As technical problems, these choices call for policy analysis.

Clearly the procurement of information is the prerequisite of policy analysis. However, clear-cut and compelling answers rarely emerge from technical policy analysis except when the problem of choice is very simple. As discussed further below, a great deal of the required information is time-consuming, expensive, and often impossible to procure. Since policy is oriented to the future, projection

[10]*Cf.* F.M. Scherer, *The Weapons Acquisition Process: Economic Incentives* (Cambridge, Mass.: Harvard University Press, 1964), p. 32.

and prediction are unavoidable even though they are extremely precarious operations; and neither national objectives and goals, nor value patterns for comparing the consequences of alternative policies, are likely to be delivered as data allowing rigorous analytical operations from which compelling answers to policy questions emerge automatically. Even regarded as a technical problem, therefore, decisions on military policy require the crucial exercise of judgment as well as the application of rigorous methods of data assembly and analysis. This is why a capacity for expert judgment as well as analytical resources for technical analysis is part of administrative skill and competence. By judgment we mean, in this context, the substantive judgment of persons who are skilful at conceptualizing the problems of choice involved, rely on technical analysis for what it is worth, and then decide on the basis of experienced, or educated, intuition.[11] An organization which has an adequate number of people possessing this kind of judgment, and which uses them to best advantage, commands an important component of administrative competence.

However, decision-making in the military sector is not only a technical problem to be solved by expertise in one form or another. There is the third major difficulty, or at any rate complication, besetting the decision-making progress. Inevitably and profoundly, this process is also a *political* problem; and its solution as a political problem requires political agreement or tolerance, and political skill in bringing agreement or tolerance about.[12] In part it is the technical limitations of policy analysis which permit politics to intrude. When the information is soft, predictions controversial and conclusions non-compelling, people can choose to reject analysis and conclusions, which they may want to do if the implications of these conclusions run counter to the interests they embody or represent. Mainly, however, politics is an essential and necessary part of making decisions on military policy because clarifying national goals and the values to be applied in policy analysis are not technical problems. These elements of the problem raise the question of what is in the public interest—an overall value on which persons inside and outside government are apt to disagree.

The political nature of the policy problem is obvious when the big questions of military policy are up for decision. If the matter is to raise the military budget, people with different interests and roles will differ in their sensitivity to the implied costs, that is, to the foregone use of resources for other purposes such as private consumption, education, and the elimination of city slums. Similarly, if the question is one of initiating or continuing war, different people will respond

[11]*Cf.* E.S. Quade, "When Quantitative Models are Inadequate," in *System Analysis and Policy Planning, Applications in Defense,* ed. E.S. Quade and W.I. Boucher (New York: American Elsivier Publishing Co., 1968), ch. 18.
[12]For the best discussion of this problem, see Charles E. Lindblom, *The Policy-Making Process* (Englewood Cliffs: Prentice-Hall, 1968), ch. 3.

differently to the value of the national objectives and of the diverse costs of achieving it. Clearly, the preferences of members of government and influential publics are more or less heterogeneous in any nation, no matter how it is organized politically. If the set of priorities directing the military effort is to embody social preferences, then the infusion of politics into policymaking is inevitable. But even when military policy turns on questions of less immediate and general political impact—when they are on the level at which getting the most military worth from given expenditures is the operative problem—different persons involved officially (*e.g.*, government departments, military services) or unofficially (*e.g.*, leaders of political parties or various special interest groups) are apt to disagree. They may do so because they differ in their conceptions of how military worth is best increased; but they may also disagree because their careers, political, and business interests diverge. Thus—whether role and professional perspective has led to conflicting perceptions of national interest or military worth, or whether competitive personal and group interests engender disagreement—navy officers may favor, and army officers oppose, policies increasing the role of the navy; R and D personnel may favor, and service personnel oppose, policies boosting the role of research and development at the expense of immediate weapon procurement; etc.

The politics of decision-making, and policy disagreement, are not necessarily unproductive. Partisanship and the insertion of special interests may not only insure proper consideration of different values to which different parts of government and public subscribe. They may also lead to competitive policy analysis and thereby enrich the flow of technical expertise brought to bear on questions of choice. Yet this is the case only where policy analysis is respected and judgment unsupported by elaborate justification is rejected.

But eventually policy decision demands agreement or tolerance, and hence the feat of persuasion, adjustment and cooperation pursued by various formal and informal procedures.[13] Therefore, the ability of the authorities to arrive at military policy by managing the politics of it in a way which is as consonant as possible with the conclusions of technical analysis and expert judgment, and which also answers to any need for dispatch, is another vital element of administrative competence. The basic skill involved here is, to be sure, political; but it is a skill which is part of the administrative effort. We therefore regard it as belonging to a nation's administrative competence in military matters.

The fourth major difficulty encountered in managing the production, maintenance, and use of national military strength of modern states results from the rapidity of change in the environment, especially the technological environment. In the course of the past two decades, accelerating progress in military technology, largely en-

[13]*Ibid.*, pp. 32 ff., 93.

gineered by military R and D, has created a situation in which the administrators of the military sector in the larger industrial states are confronted with an obsolescence of weapons and forces proceeding at a truly alarming rate, and—this is the central problem—with an alarming number of possible choices in developing new weapon systems. The pace of change and the sheer numerical complexity of the technological options borders on the overwhelming. In addition, the non-technological environment is also changing rapidly and often unexpectedly. In large part resulting ultimately from the process of economic and industrial development spreading across the earth, political realities seem unprecedentedly in flux, and their change keeps reshaping the international environment within which national military power is designed to operate.

The exigencies of technological change make, as we have seen in Chapter III, military R and D a key activity in the leading industrial states. Technological uncertainty makes it inadvisable to proceed immediately to the production of weapon systems. The purpose of R and D, in its initial phases, is in fact to widen and classify the range of technological options open for serving military ends. As development costs mount in subsequent phases, the options are narrowed. When a procurement decision is made, R and D has served the function of dispelling, or at least reducing, uncertainty about what weapons to produce. Especially in areas in which the technological choices are many, large and expensive, this is the central purpose of military R and D.

But it is not only in R and D that, in the modern world, administrative resilience is the hallmark of successful military management. As already observed, changes in the external politico-military world demand a continuous review, and may necessitate adjustment in procurement, tables of organization, military strategy, and doctrine. Furthermore, the volume of resources available to the military sector is apt to change with changes in overall productive capacity and the pressure of other demands for resources. Also, the values on which foreign-policy objectives are based, and which sustain the national willingness to use force, may undergo gradual change, Finally, the fact that planning assumptions about the future (e.g., the capabilities and behavior of allies and opponents) may turn out to have been more or less wrong may call for alterations in military forces, etc. The process of organizing national military forces and power—based as it must be at any one time on a set of hypothetical assumptions about the future—is a continuous operation of testing reality, a learning process of directing adaptation.

For all these reasons, flexibility is a major asset, especially in this very dynamic world. By investing in versatility, operational flexibility can be built, to some extent, into the structure of the armed forces, and into military strategy and doctrine. But managerial adaptiveness is the principal asset. Administrative flexibility consists of a firm disposition to obtain as accurate a perception of the changing world as possible and a propensity which, in response to changes in the environment, reexamines the premises from which military policy is derived, explores new options, and innovates whenever possible in order to improve the ingredients of national military strength.[14] The demands for adaptation of course enter the political process involved in administrative decision-making. Policy adaptation is apt to disadvantage some interest groups and promise to benefit others.

These, then, are the principal components of military administrative potential: competence in policy analysis, expert judgment, flexibility, and skill in managing the politics of military decision-making.

Tools of Policy Analysis

Having identified the four chief components of administrative skill, it is worthwhile to discuss one of these, the technical capacity for policy analysis in more detail, since there has been since World War II an unprecedented burgeoning of resources appropriate to this activity. The vastly improved means of technical analysis reduce the need to rely on judgment or, at any rate, make judgment more educated; policy analysis has also penetrated the world of political partisanship concerned with military policy; finally, policy analysis also makes a vital contribution to the exercise of administrative flexibility.

The analytical tools now available for policy analysis give far more sharpness to the job of relating means to ends than was formerly possible.[15] There is operations research, pioneered during World War II, which employs various techniques to seek, whenever feasible, to quantify the merits and demerits of alternative policy solutions to a problem. Thus, a military aircraft under development can be designed to have more range, speed, radar equipment and bomb load; if it is possible to show quantitatively how much speed must be sacrificed for how much range, or how much range for how much radar or bomb load, and how different combinations effect the cost of production and operations, various trade-offs between the values involved are established, and this provides a basis for making a decision affording optimum results. Systems analysis, which incorporates the methods of operations research, extends the examination to an elucidation of operational objectives. To return to the illustration just used, the systems analyst may introduce strategic considerations which indicate the relative value of speed versus range, or range versus "pay load," The heart of these analytical methods is the cost-benefit or cost-effectiveness approach. It begins with conceptualizing a problem

[14]*Cf.* Paul Y. Hammond, "A Functional Analysis of Defense Department Decision-Making in the McNamera Administration," *The American Political Science Review,* LXII (March 1968), p. 66.
[15]See the various chapters in *Defense Management,* ed. Enke, and *Systems Analysis and Policy Planning,* ed. Quade and Boucher.

of choice. This means construction of an analytical model which specifies the relations between various inputs (costs) and outputs (values). Once the relevant properties of a problem are laid bare, alternative solutions are compared systematically in terms of financial costs or in terms of all inputs of scarce resources. The problem is to find a solution for which financial costs or the use of other resources is minimized for a given military effect. Other techniques of policy analysis are linear and dynamic programming, decision theory, gaming, and simulation. At the service of these techniques is a vastly expanded capability, supplied by the new technology for processing information, to handle huge masses of data with great speed, accuracy and economy.

In the United States, the use of these new techniques was introduced rigorously in the Defense Department by Mr. McNamara (1961–68). The new administrative procedures restructured the demands of the military services in terms of distinct military missions so that it became possible to compare proposed costs with promised accomplishment, and also put planning on a longer-term basis than the one-year measure which had made it difficult, in any one fiscal year, to choose with reference to the cumulative benefits and costs of any particular military program. The new instrument for formal planning was called Planning-Programming-Budgeting (PPB)[16] which was installed in 1961. PPB provides for a five-year planning structure and process in order to guide the formulation of annual budgets. The entire scope of defense activities is classified into individual programs, such as the Polaris submarine or army divisions, and then grouped into major programs: strategic nuclear forces, general-purpose forces, etc. Manpower, weapons, and financial planning levels are proposed and then reviewed by means of systems analysis, for each part of these programs. For these purposes, the Department of Defense relied not only on its own administrative facilities, but— especially with regard to difficult problems of R and D—also upon the resources of universities and various independent research organizations.

The introduction of these new administrative methods amounted to a major management revolution. This new and expanding family of analytical techniques is essentially part of the accelerating process of scientific and technological progress. Science and technology are not only transforming national economies; they are also transforming government and administration. The methods are basically scientific; their purpose is to increase knowledge by replicable means; and they lend themselves to making administrative decision-making as long as the activity is regarded as a problem of rationally evaluating and exercising choices between alternatives.

These new tools are of no avail, of course, if a decision-maker prefers, or is induced by circumstances beyond his control, to act

[16]Cf. Charles J. Hitch, *Decision-Making for Defense* (Berkely: University of California Press, 1965).

irrationally, or at a low level of rationality—except that irrational choices may show up starkly against a background of policy analysis. And, as indicated earlier, these techniques have limitations when applied to administrative decision-making proceeding at a high level of rationality.

One limitation relates to insufficiency of information about present and past. Military planners, for example, may not know with any degree of confidence about the decisions (*e.g.,* on R and D) which their opposite numbers in potentially hostile states have made or are making. More importantly, since decisions on military production or R and D will come to fruition only with a considerable time lag, sometimes stretching to eight or ten years, they are made with reference to a future environment which it is always hard and in many respects impossible to predict. Technology itself is difficult to predict even if one disregards true "breakthroughs." Time and costs required by military development and production are hard to predict, as the administrative record bears out most eloquently. Essentially unpredictable is the behavior in international crises of other states, and other aspects of the evolving politico-military environment.[17] To be sure, analytical techniques have also been developed to make reasonably good conjectures about the future.[18] Trend analysis based on the cautious projection ahead of current trends, the concept of designing alternative possible futures, and the technique, whenever useful, to confine prediction to types of phenomena (*e.g.,* types of conflicts, opponents, theaters of war) rather than individual phenomena are proving helpful[19] and are capable of further refinement.

There are administrative problems of a relative simplicity in which these problems of prediction are absent or insignificant, or in which present techniques of conjecturing give satisfactory results. Yet they are unable to inspire confidence when it comes to the more consequential decisions in the military sector. To give an example, some years ago, the United States Department of Defense made a decision (since revised) to build conventionally-fueled rather than more nuclear-powered aircraft carriers. The former were cheaper to produce and it was decided that the operational advantages of the nuclear carrier did not justify the difference in costs. To make this decision with any degree of confidence, one had to be reasonably sure that political and military situations placing a premium on the advantages of the nuclear carrier were unlikely to arise, or were not important enough if they did arise, to spend more money on carriers. But these are precisely the kinds of "predictions" that cannot be made with any degree of confidence.

[17]*Cf.* Klaus Knorr and Oskar Morgenstern, *Political Conjecture in Military Planning,* Princeton University, Center of International Studies, Policy Memorandum No. 35 (1968), pp. 10–15.

[18]*Cf.* T.J. Gordon and Olaf Helmer, *Report on a Long-Range Forecasting Study,* RAND paper P-2982 (September 1964); "Toward the Year 2000: Work in Progress," *Daedalus* (Summer 1967); *Futuribles,* ed. Bertrand de Jouvenel (Geneva: Droz, 1963).

[19]Knorr and Morgenstern, *Political Conjecture in Military Planning,* pp. 21–35.

Thus, workable criteria have been elaborated to solve problems at the level of "sub-optimization" which, as in the solution of logistic problems, permit a specific objective to be maximized in terms of inputs, although even here feasibility and results depend on the skill and imagination of the analyst in identifying and relating the important variables, and on adequate information. At higher levels of choice, however, cost-benefit analysis and PPB face formidable problems because the outputs which can be derived from various combinations of inputs, are not the same and, being unmeasurable, are difficult to evaluate comparatively. Looking at the military effort as a whole, the process of maximizing military worth from a given volume of resource inputs involves a vast aggregate of heterogeneous assets whose usability is more or less uncertain. The nature of military worth would be difficult enough to discover in a world of tested and unchanging (or very slowly changing) weapons systems. But contemporary decisions are made in a universe of weapons systems which are largely untested and, moreover, subject to a stupendous rate of obsolescence. Even if one's criteria of efficiency are made less rigorous, as when one is satisfied with more rather than less "satisfactory" solutions, the essential difficulties remain.

On top of these limitations, the use of the new tools of policy analysis are, of course, subject to degradation as a result of administrative malpractices. For instance, if parts of policy analysis are quantitative and other parts are not, there is some risk that the act of decision-making pays exaggerated heed to the quantitative parts of the analysis which looks neat and definitive (although even this may be deceptive if poor data were used) while the rest of the analysis sounds speculative and often vague.[20] Various other procedures may grow to importance even though they are untested and often faulty.[21] There is the involvement of politics which leads to the introduction of various forms of bias even in the application of the new techniques.[22] Finally, systems analysis is apt to exaggerate the virtue of logical consistence in analysis and conclusions while oversimplifying assumptions about a very "rich" environment and deemphasizing the need for reviewing these premises.[23]

If the new management tools can be used well or badly, results patently depend on the skill and wisdom with which their employment is directed and exploited. The techniques themselves, for instance, tell us nothing about the nature of military strength, and the utility of its uses. The cost-effectiveness approach, if applied without imagination and restraint, can be stifling especially in military R and

---

[20]Klaus Knorr, "On the Cost-Effectiveness Approach to Military Research and Development," *Bulletin of Atomic Scientists*, November 1966, pp. 11–14.
[21]*Cf.* Robert L. Perry, *The Mythography of Military R and D*, RAND paper P-3356 (May 1966).
[22]James R. Schlesinger, *Systems Analysis and the Political Process*, RAND paper P-3464 (June 1967).
[23]Hammond, *op. cit.*, p. 67.

D,[24] or regarding any problems calling for innovation.[25] A style of management rigidly devoted to economy and efficiency, with particular emphasis on minimizing financial costs, may dispel the institutional climate in which innovation prospers. This danger is compounded by the fact that, the new methods and resources of policy analysis apart, public administration has resisted innovation. It remains structured along traditional hierarchial lines. Indeed, progress in the social sciences has rather bypassed the area of public administration.[26]

Despite these limitations of the new analytical tools, and the administrative abuse to which they, like all instruments, can be put, any rational decision-maker will be eager to employ them for all they are worth, which is evidently a great deal. Without these techniques, decision-makers are doomed to move far more in the dark, and in the fog of uncertainties, than is necessary at this time. And their value will probably rise as, with cumulating experience, the administrative *art* of applying these *scientific* methods is gradually improved.

There are a number of other administrative techniques or expedients which the administrator in the military sector will practice as do administrators in other parts of government, or in non-public institutions. The use of policy feedback, and of policy experiment are among these.[27] Reliance on feed back is a patently important method for insuring flexibility. But one aid to policy analysis and decision-making which, in the military sector requires special attention, is ideology.[28]

Ideology is a set of interrelated beliefs generalizing about relevant parts and properties of the environment. Such beliefs are apt to enter the decision-making process whether they are loose or rigid, fragmentary or comprehensive, formal or informal, and regardless of whether or not the actors are conscious of the fact that they subscribe to an ideology in this sense. Administrators and politicans anywhere are more or less subject to such beliefs which may concern the nature of their own state, and its political and economic system. They may also concern the nature and value of science and technology. In the administration of the military sector, they may concern the character of the external environment, the nature, capabilities and motivations of opponents and allies, the nature of military power, the utility of military force in serious crises, and so forth. From our present point of view, it is important to note that ideologies—which are dominant among a set of decision-makers—affect the context of policy analysis, inform administrative judgment, and impinge on related political

[24]*Cf.* Paul J. Sturm, "Problem Mongers, Solution Mongers and Weapon System Effectiveness," *Defense Industry Bulletin*, II (July 1966), pp. 1–4.
[25]Victor A. Thompson, "How Scientific Management Thwarts Innovation," *Transaction*, June 1968, pp. 51–54.
[26]*Ibid.*, p. 52.
[27]*Cf.* Lindblom, *op. cit.*, pp. 24–27.
[28]*Ibid.*, pp. 23–24.

activities. This influence does not, of course, exclude, although it restricts the sway of, pragmatic considerations. This administrative function of ideology is to help coordinate administrative activities by providing various *assumptions* on objectives, means and environment, which are either accepted as a matter of course or about which argument is narrowly circumscribed. It does so particularly regarding premises which it would be difficult, if not impossible, to verify by analysis. On this view, ideology does not take the place of analysis but provides it with a degree of guidance. Dominant ideologies may, of course, be revised over time—because of new perceptions evoked by ill-fitting events or, indeed, by analysis. But the change is usually gradual.

It follows that, in affecting decisions on military forces and their use, the weight of ideological assumptions will be the greater, the more commonly and rigidly they are held, and the more comprehensive they are about the relevant environment. It likewise follows that the quality of the administrative decisions depends on the degree to which these assumptions conform to the nature of the real world. All these properties of ideology are a question of more or less in all states. Ideology is, of course, much more formal, comprehensive and assertive in the communist states than, for example, in western democratic countries. This fact does not necessarily prove that ideology is unchangingly influential in Communistic countries and, in actual administration, pragmatic considerations and policy analysis may play their considerable role. Similarly, the fact that many Americans believe that they are free of ideology does not, of course mean that they are. It means only that they do not regard sets of assumptions about reality as ideology and that they are confirmed in this view by the lack of formality accorded to these assumptions.

International Comparison

Administrative skills are indubitably important in the production (and use) of national military strength and, indeed, can be critical in the generation of international power. Government intelligence services are therefore forced to appraise these capabilities in other countries as best they can. As defined in this study, however, administrative competence as a whole, or in most of its parts, does not lend itself to precise measurement and hence to rigorous international comparison. Even in retrospect, unless differences are gross, it is hard to compare administrative performance because of the difficulty of separating the impact of this one factor from the totality of factors which determined the outcome of military clashes between states.

How, for instance, should we measure the supply and use of expert judgment, or the skills involved in managing administrative flexibility and the politics of decisionmaking in the military sector? In the absence of a workable theory of public administration, there are no methods for doing so. Nor have social scientists so far discovered good indicators, that is, phenomena which are visible and measurable, on the one hand, and reasonably representative of various components of administrative competence, on the other hand—as GNP and R and D budgets are indicators of economic and technological capacity. One could not, for instance, compare the efficiency of R and D administration by relating moneys spent on abandoned projects to total R and D outlays. A comparison of states along this line would ignore the facts that some states tried more difficult and innovative projects, or deliberately bought more insurance against a technologically uncertain future, or derived more valuable by-products in technological knowhow, than other states did.

A further difficulty is that the process of administrative decision-making in the military sector is more or less covered by secrecy in many states. To the extent that this is the case, the study of administrative capabilities in other public sectors might commend itself as an alternative. However, aside from the fact that the lack of measurability applies to administrative performance in other sectors as well, it cannot be assumed that the administrative competence of governments is evenly spread over all areas of activity. For example, the fact that Soviet economic planning is characterized by conspicuous bureaucratic deficiencies,[29] does not necessarily mean that Soviet decision-making on military matters is subject to the same weaknesses or, if so, to the same extent. It would certainly have been a mistake to infer the administrative competence of the Department of Defense in the United States, from 1961 to 1968, from the administrative performance of the Departments of Commerce or State. This is not to deny that, in particular states, government bureaucracy across the board may not suffer from general deficiencies, or exhibit certain general strengths, which also affect the management of the military effort in these states. For instance, the relative ease with which federal administration in the United States permits recruitment, and employs advisers and consultants, at various levels in the hierarchy, from a number of skills (e.g., scientists and economists), encourages variety in administrative approaches to problem-solving, impedes bureaucratic rigidification, and greatly enriches the administrative resources brought to bear on defense planning. This kind of mobility of talent and skills under government auspices has been more difficult to accomodate in England where civil servants traditionally start at the bottom and work their way slowly up the ladder, or in West Germany which suffers from an extreme degree of departmental autonomy and excessive reliance on personnel trained in the law.[30] Unfortunately, however, there is not tested general knowledge on how differences in administrative inputs are related to differences in output; and this constitutes a formidable barrier to generalization and comparison.

Only regarding one administrative resource—the use of policy

[29]*Cf.* Joseph S. Berliner, "Russia's Bureaucrats—Why They Are Reactionary," *Transaction,* December 1967, pp. 53–58.
[30]Klaus Seemann, "Beamte ausder Retorte," *Die Zeit,* April 2, 1968, p. 8.

analysis—is it possible to offer a plausible generalization. The more the purpose and merit of policy analysis are appreciated in a country over the whole range of administrative functions, in business as well as in government, the greater the supply of resources for policy analysis, and the more this supply is growing in response to demand, the more likely it is that these resources will be also in demand in the military sector. A prerequisite for such a situation is a high level of education and a flourishing of the social sciences, mathematics, statistics, and computer technology, and a strong commitment to the value of science.

The question arises whether, even if it is difficult or impossible to draw meaningful comparisons of administrative competence between individual countries, it is not feasible to compare *types* of states in this respect. It might be asked, for example, whether "communist" and "capitalist" states, though differing markedly within each group in the way government and economy are organized, are not each as a group, superior to the other in all, some, or one of the components of administrative competence we have identified as important determinants of output in the military sector of society. Indeed, it is easy to think of interesting propositions and questions. For example, it would seem that ideological commitments in the Communist countries have obstructed the development of certain disciplines (notably economics) in ways which handicap systems analysis as practiced in the United States. Or it might be asked how differences in political ideology might influence military planning in the two groups of countries. If ideology about the political nature of the outside world were unrealistic, and commitment to this ideology rigid, in communist states while non-communist states were free of ideologies distorting the perception of the external environment, one would expect— everything else being the same—the military strength of the latter countries to be more appropriate to foreign-policy demands than is the case in the former countries. Yet we simply do no know whether dominant ideologies in the government of, for instance, the United States are more realistic than those in the government of, for example, the Soviet Union. Nor do we know whether political ideology plays actually more of a role in the administration of the Soviet military sector than in that of the American.

Neither the historical record nor speculation permits us to rank these classes of countries in terms of administrative competence simply on the basis of their general form of organization. It is safer to assume that—though constraints and restraints associated with general forms of government of economic system *may* influence administrative performance—it is *particular* administrative leaders, structures, and procedures which dominate administrative performance.[31] This assumption would lead one to expect that administrative competence in the military sector can be high or low in either set of states,

[31]*Cf. Knorr,* The War Potential of Nations, p. 158.

and that it is subject to change, for other reasons than change of political or economic system, in any one state of either set.

There is, however, one way of classifying states which permits considerable generalization about administrative capacity. This is a classification in terms of relative "modernization" or, to be more specific, in terms of economic, technological, and scientific development. Viewing the history of states now "modern," it is clear that they have at present a far greater ability to mobilize political, social, and economic resources to serve public ends than they possessed in pre-modern times, and that they also enjoy now more administrative flexibility than they did formerly.[32] It is equally clear that expanding education and research have led in these states to the development of the resources required for policy analysis. Finally, where education and free research flourished one would expect a tendency for unrealistic ideologies to be challenged and eventually revised.

Foreign Procurement

For the reasons just given, one would expect the economically less developed states to have, as a class, a distinctly low competence for administering their military sector efficiently. However, though this would seem to be generally true—always subject, however, to differences resulting from special factors such as personal leadership—this fact does not render this set of countries militarily helpless. To the extent that they import sophisticated military equipment—which, as a class, they do—they obviously do not require the administrative competence which has led to the design and production of this equipment. In a sense, they import administrative knowhow embodied in the hardware. Reliance on foreign training for military personnel, or on advice from foreign experts serves the same function.

Of course, the possibility of importation does not, if only for political reasons, extend to the entire range of military planning. Political and military authorities must make many decisions which affect the amount and kind of military strength they are able to generate. Administrative competence is a critical capability also in these countries.

[32]*Cf.* Paul Y. Hammond, "The Political Order and the Burden of External Relations," *World Politics,* XIX (April 1967), p. 459.

5 The Political Foundations of Military Power

For a nation to increase its military effort, it must not only possess economic, technological, and administrative resources; it must first of all have the will to do so. A government decided on increasing the state's military effort must have or receive the authority to allocate the necessary resources. Whatever else it is, the mobilization of military potential is also *political* mobilization.[1] On extracting from society available resources which a government deems necessary for the purpose, the limiting factor is essentially political. Where this limit will be placed depends both upon situational factors and, as pointed out in Chapter II, on predispositional factors which are antecedent to the situation, and which we regard as the state's political military potential. These two sets of factors must be clearly distinguished from one another. In order to clarify the distinction, we will briefly identify the conditions which determine the willingness and ability of a government to mobilize additional resources for the purpose of augmenting or improving the armed forces of the state (or for the purpose of employing these forces internationally).

Governments may, of course, want to increase military forces for various *domestic* purposes, including that of suppressing opposition and insuring government control. But the present study is not concerned with this range of objectives; and they are therefore excluded from the analysis.

Given the focus of this study, the willingness of a government to

[1]Paul Y. Hammond, "The Political Order and the Burden of External Relations," *World Politics*, XIX (April 1967), pp. 443–449.

increase a state's military effort depends, first, on its foreign-policy goals; second, on stimuli received from the outside world, that is, on the perception of threats which may be warded off or of opportunities to press foreign-policy goals by military means; third, on means-end calculations, that is, on decisions about the magnitude or structure of military forces, on the international uses of military capabilities, which are required by foreign-policy goals in the perceived situations; and fourth, on the government's estimated ability to extract the necessary resources for the military sector—or in the case of the international use of force, the government's domestic ability to secure the commitment to such employment.

The present study is not concerned with the first condition, even though the generation of foreign-policy goals and objectives is related to the actual and potential military strength of states. The second and the third conditions clearly depend on the particular situation facing the government making a choice of action. The fourth condition is partly situational and partly predispositional, and hence must be further differentiated. The domestic support which a government commands or receives—whether strong or weak—is also in part situational. To the extent that members of the public take interest in, and have influence on, such a policy, they lend more or less support partly as a result of notions on foreign-policy goals, reactions to events on the outside world, and ideas about means and ends, which they or their representatives have. In these considerations, they may be influenced by the information made available by the government, as well as by independent mass media and other resources of information. But if they take interest in the policy in question, their considerations may coincide with, or more or less diverge from, those of government. Whatever the result, it will tend to affect the degree and kind of support given to the government on the matter in question.

Whether these situational responses of the public are effective depends, of course, on the political system of the state concerned, on the degree to which public responses are united or divided, and—if divided—on the structure of domestic political influence. However, whenever the question of public support is meaningful, it is also a consequence of predispositional factors which may be more determinative of public support than the situational considerations, and which in fact may influence the situational considerations themselves. The antecedent conditions are: the nation's propensity to mobilize military force and use it internationally; the public predisposition to support the national community; the public's predisposition to support the government's foreign and military policy; and support of this policy for reasons of particular personal and group interest.

Clearly, these antecedent attitudes and interests are apt to affect the situational responses. Thus, members of the public who have a high propensity to favor the use of force internationally will perceive particular international conflict situations and undertake particular means-ends calculations in these terms. Or the military who, like all specialists, favor the employment of their specialist skills, or who foresee career and other personal and group advantages from an expansion of the armed forces, are also likely to perceive and interpret international relationships in a manner favoring these attitudes and interests.

However, situational responses need not be influenced or dominated by antecedent attitudes and interests. For example, even people with a high predisposition to favor the international use of force on behalf of their country's interests may be against any *particular* occasion or policy for increasing or improving the armed forces. They may oppose a particular use of force because they expect it to entail disastrous consequences to their country, or for some other reason. They may oppose a particular proposal for raising the military budget because they prefer alternative uses for the public funds involved. Moreover, as we shall see, predispositions may be differentiated in various ways, favoring an expansionist military policy only for certain kinds of international conflict situations, and not for others. We only maintain that the antecedent factors of which a nation's political military potential is composed condition situational responses. Given various kinds of international conflict situations, a nation with strong predilections in favor of military action will tend to react differently from a nation given to the opposite predilections.

National Propensity to Use Military Power

Nations have differed throughout history, and nations differ at the present time, in the basic readiness with which they resort to military force in the event of interstate conflict or on behalf of acquisitive foreign-policy goals. They differ in being "warlike" or "peaceable." In the 1930's, most observers ranked Germany and Japan in terms of this disposition far above France and the United States; and just before World War II, Finland and Poland ranked in this respect above Czechoslovakia. Even though they were vastly inferior in numbers, Finland fought the Soviet Union, and Poland fought Nazi Germany; but Czechoslovakia yielded to Germany's military might without fighting. In the middle 1960's, many observers would have ranked the United States and the Soviet Union in this respect above Japan and Great Britain. Over time, many states have undergone substantial change in this disposition.

A nation with a high propensity to mobilize military strength and to apply it against other countries is relatively appreciative of the advantages of using force, and relatively insensitive to the disadvantages or costs. Like any attitude, this predisposition combines elements of affect and cognition. The affective components constitute a feeling of like or dislike, whether feeble or strong, toward military force and war. The cognitive components constitute a set of beliefs about these objects of like or dislike. If these beliefs are part of a more or less consistent system and consciously held, they amount to an ideology, or part of an ideological complex. A person or group which has a pronounced disposition toward military power and its use may, of course, value only some of the typical advantages and appreciate many of the typical disadvantages in terms of affect and cognition. Various constellations of particular likes and dislikes are possible. For example, a society may have a high predisposition to use force in self-defense, but not in support of acquisitive objectives. The propensity may vary considerably in strength with reference to different types of international situations. In any case, the predisposition held by persons or groups is a *net* attitude, composed of positive and negative components.

Within a nation, or any sub-group, the propensity of different individual members may differ more or less in terms of direction, scope, and intensity. Thus, regarding intensity, the military officer class is apt to have a higher propensity to support the build-up and use of force than the rest of the population, in which some groups may be intensely dedicated to pacifism. In the nineteenth-century history of France and Germany, right-wing political parties were motivated by a strong propensity to the use of military force, whereas left-wing, especially socialist, parties usually subscribed to a pacifist creed. Just before World War I, anti-military and anti-war sentiment was voiced vigorously by socialist leaders in France and Germany. Regarding scope, some members of the public may favor the use of force over a broad spectrum of international conflicts, including military aggression, while others are opposed to all use of force, and still others are disposed to support only its defensive employment. Concerning direction, some members may be more inclined to favor force against some country or countries, but less so, or not at all, against others. Some American Jews, for instance, may favor United States military support of Israel, if necessary for her survival, while opposing other kinds of military involvement on the part of the United States. Similarly, Communist party members in West European states are apt to oppose any moblization of military strength, even purely defensive, vis-a-vis the Soviet Union; but they might favor such mobilization against a country designated by Communist leaders as "imperialist" or "fascist." The disposition to support military policy may thus be more or less differentiated. When we speak of a nation being "warlike" or "peaceable," we refer to a modal distribution in the population. The impact of this public disposition, whatever it is, depends, of course, on how its distribution in the population is related to the distribution of political influence—its elites having more influence than the mass of the population in this regard as in many others.

Various kinds of historical experience can modify national predispositions to support military force. A series of crushing defeats may do so; or the embrace of new, perhaps revolutionary, ideologies which appreciate the symbols of peace and deprecate those of war; or the rise in power of a social class or political party with a distinctly different attitude toward international force. National economic, technological and scientific development, once it reaches an advanced stage, is probably a crucial experience in this respect. Most societies have inherited a traditional, and usually positive, valuation of force from the tribal past. Over the centuries, scientific progress and educational advance have tended to corrode these traditional attitudes in the economically very developed societies; and aristocratic families, descended from a warrior caste, which have been notable carriers of these traditional values in the past, have ceased to exert special political influence or have themselves adopted the different values of modern urbanized culture. This is not to say that advanced "modernization" is sure to eliminate a high propensity to resort to arms internationally. But to the extent that "modernization" means education, a questioning spirit, and an insistence on the pragmatic application of new knowledge, it tends to diminish inherited attitudes, and thus probably increases the weight of the situational factors in the determination of national military policy. Problem-solving, which is inspired by a scientific bent, would tend in this direction.

Support of the National Community

The public predisposition to support the community contained in a soverign state consists of a sense of solidarity, sometimes called patriotism, which is love of one's country. This attitude denotes some degree of identification of self with nation (varying with different individuals and collectivities), and hence some disposition to serve the community's needs, as well as one's own. Support of the community implies political cohesion and therefore presupposes that members have achieved a high and stable level of political integration. The level of mutual trust and loyalty implied depends on the sharing of appropriate norms including criteria for establishing membership in the collectivity. Historically, foreign military challenge and war have especially tended to activate this sence of solidarity. Slogans such as "rallying around the flag," "closing ranks," "pulling together," and "political bi-partisanship" verbalize the activation of this predisposition. Indeed, the relationship between the activation of solidarity and war has been so close in the past that domestically insecure rulers, governments and elites have sometimes sought and resorted to interstate violence for the purpose of uniting a divided community and thereby strengthening their domestic position.[2] This

[2]There is some statistical evidence for this; see Jonathan Wilkenfield, "Domestic and Foreign Conflict Behavior of Nations," *Journal of Peace Research*, I (1968), pp. 56–68.

has been an important way in which international resort to force serves the domestic needs of some elites.

Despite the frequent activation of this disposition to support the national community in time of war, it is quite distinct from the propensity to favor military action, although the two attitudes can, of course, coincide in presence and strength. A sense of national solidarity can find many expressions, and will affect political life in time of peace as well as in war. Its object differs essentially from the object of supporting military action. Even though group solidarity is usually based on limited membership, and on seeing outsiders as different from fellow members in some sense, it need not produce, or be associated with, pugnacity toward other groups.

Although such group solidarity—and particularly the overriding obligation to stop internal feuding in the face of external enemies—has deep historical roots,[3] the critical question from the viewpoint of this study is whether or not, and the extent to which, it characterizes the entire population of the state and welds it into a "nation."

Like the predisposition to support military force, this sense of solidarity, and the condition of "nationhood," is highly variable within, in a state, depending on numerous factors and circumstances. For example, "nationhood" was largely lacking in eighteenth-century Europe, and did not become a significant political force before, ushered in by the French revolution, a spreading nationalism gave the west European states a new broadly-based political solidarity. This "nationalism" which is a creed centering loyalty on the "nation-state," was associated with notions of popular sovereignty. However, because and to the extent that this idea of popular sovereignty was not implemented in political constitution and practice, European nationalism before World War I was primarily a creed adopted and propagated by the upper and middle classes, and resisted by the socialist parties of Europe. If the mass of the population in Britain, France, and Germany evinced nevertheless an intensely nationalist mood in 1914, this sense of solidarity became deeply corroded in Germany during the 1920's, and in France during the 1930's.

Thus, a sense of national solidarity, once established, is subject to dissipation when deep political cleavages open up between classes and political parties, and nationhood is, of course, capable of common decline if members give priority to incompatible values. A spreading growth of narrow self-concern or the evolution, in the opposite direction, of transnational values and attitudes, transcending identification with the nation state, diminish solidarity.

Nationhood as a broadly based political force is more or less absent from most contemporary states. In several Latin American countries (*e.g.,* Peru, Ecuador, Columbia), it has never developed more than a narrow base because very sizeable parts of the pop-

---

[3]*Cf.* E.E. Evans-Pritchard, *The Nuer* (London: 1940), p. 123.

ulation have never become politically integrated within a national framework. "Nationhood" is also weak in many of the new states of Africa and Asia where group loyalty remains largely focused on tribal or local institutions and does not extend at all, or extends only feebly, to the institution of the state. Thus, nationhood is fragmentary in countries such as Burma, Tanzania, and the Congo. But viewing the economically less developed countries as a whole, there are considerable differences in this respect. There is, at the present time, a great deal more "nationhood" in Algeria, the United Arab Republic, and Turkey than, for example, in Malaysia, Thailand, and Cyprus; and there is more in China than in India. In many of the countries of recent colonial origin that are existing at a low level of economic development, nationhood is only beginning to come into its own.

Predisposition to Support Government Policy

The third type of predisposition is a tendency to support the government's foreign and military policy regardless of specific content, that is, to support it simply because it is the government's policy. Such support for a government's policy to allocate more resources to the military sector, or to apply military power internationally, rests on the public's acceptance of government policy as an authoritative or legitimate act. To the extent that government enjoys such authority, its policy is accepted without justification in terms of specific merit.

Complete acceptance of government decisions as authoritative does not, of course, occur in any state and any situation. Normally, if governments want their policies supported, they must persuade some or most groups of the population that the proposed course of action has merit; or they must bargain by offering some groups some sort of *quid pro quo;* or, in some systems, they may have to compel support. Some groups, and perhaps many individuals, may simply be indifferent to all government policy, or to foreign and military policy in particular; and indifference must not be confused with support. And some groups will usually remain opposed to the policy, openly or silently. What is at issue is the degree to which a proportion of the public support the government's military policy, and feel themselves bound by it, simply because it is issued by legitimate authority.

There have been numerous indications in western countries that the general public pays ordinarily little attention to foreign and military policy or, which is more relevant to our discussion, is ordinarily disposed to accept such policy as a matter of course.[4] And

[4]*Cf.* Gabriel A. Almond and Sidney Verba, *The Civic Culture* (Princeton: Princeton University Press, 1963), Part II; Warren E. Miller and Donald E. Stokes, "Constituency Influence in Congress," *American Political Science Review,* LVII (1963), pp. 45–56; *Domestic Sources of Foreign Policy,* ed. James N. Rosenau (New York Free Press, 1967), pp. 24–30, also Ch. VII.

it is not rare in these countries that legislative bodies vote almost automatically for defense expenditures proposed by the executive branch of government.

Yet there have been as many indications in these countries that unquestioning support, and indifference, begin to cease with an increasing number of the public as soon as serious and direct sacrifices are demanded from them and their impact on individual interests is perceived.[5] This tends to happen when taxes are increased, more men drafted into the armed services or, in the event of war, when casualties occur. The shifting attitude of the American people in the course of the wars in Korea and Vietnam present eloquent testimony to this effect. As soon as the public raises questions about the government's military policy, the type of support under discussion diminishes or ceases to operate. Questioning does not, however, mean necessarily that public support declines. A questioning public may give support but, in that case, support originates in considerations of the pros and cons and will be strongly affected by the perceptions of situational conditions.

The question may be asked whether public interest in foreign and military policy tends to rise with a rising level of education combined with augmented sources of information, such as radio and television. If this is true, it means that public indifference declines. It does not mean necessarily that the acceptance of government military policy as authoritative is automatically underminded. However, with an increasing public interest in foreign and military policy one would expect an increased influence of public considerations based on the perception and evaluation of *situational* factors.

The public disposition to accept and support the government's military policy without examination of its substantive merit may be based not only on the fact that it issues from authority, regardless of the persons holding office, but also, under special circumstances, on the qualities of particular leaders. Throughout history, certain leaders—*e.g.,* Napoleon, Hitler, Nehru, Mao Tse-tung, Churchill— have achieved a high degree of personal authority which caused many of their followers to accept their policies without question.

In conclusion, the type of support in question is—in terms of strength, scope, and distribution in the public—a variable which is sensitive to a variety of conditions.

Support Inspired by Interest

Finally, there is a type of predispositional support which results from the direct and abiding interest of some individuals and groups in any

---

[5]*Cf.* Kenneth W. Waltz, "Electoral Punishment and Foreign Policy Crises," in *Domestic Sources of Foreign Policy,* ed. Rosenau, Ch. X.

government policy of mobilizing or employing military strength. We are not concerned here with policy support which the government, in appropriate situations, bargains for by offering advantages and concessions, as for example, when a government undertakes or promises certain domestic reforms in order to obtain a broader base of support. We are rather concerned with cases in which certain members of the public perceive to have a direct interest in armaments or the international use of force. The main cases are when such policies are expected to further career interests (especially among military officers) or business interests (particularly enterprises expecting contracts to produce weapons and other military supplies). When President Eisenhower spoke and warned of the "military-industrial complex" which had developed in the United States during the 1950's, he was referring to interest-groups of this kind. That the professional military and specialized armament industries should have such interests should be no cause of surprise. Nor is it to be assumed that their members are greedy "merchants of death," etc. They are apt to share, often particularly so, the attitudes discussed previously, such as strong support of community.

There is also a more subtle form of self-interest, capable of satisfaction by an expansive military policy. In earlier historical eras and especially in mankind's tribal past, entire populations were more or less conditioned by cultural norms extolling the waging of war. To the extent that these kinds of norms remained effective, government policy aiming at increasing or employing military strength conferred psychological income on the people attached to such values. This was strikingly true in Japan during the 1930's. There is little of this cultural attachment to military enterprise left in the modern world, and virtually none in the highly developed countries. There are, however, and have been numerous cases of strong domestic interest in measures for strengthening the state militarily *vis-à-vis* a particular foreign country, often a neighboring state which is regarded as a "hereditary" enemy. Frenchmen dreaming of *revanche* against Germany after the War of 1870–71, and the feelings between Greeks and Turks and between Arabs and Israelis in recent decades, are examples. Such feelings are precipitated by personalized historical experience; they are not created by propaganda at a time of crisis. They make for a self-interest in a pursuit of national military strength which is antecedent to any particular international crisis. It is arguable that these feelings should be excluded from the type of predisposition discussed in this section because they are not general or diffuse, and are therefore unable to generate support for any but very specific government policies involving the mobilization or use of military power. However, in most instances, particularly those involving lesser military powers, where specific animosities are directed against *practically* the only object of maintaining, enlarging, and employing military forces, such feelings practically coincide with a more diffuse predisposition.

Political Military Potential

The four predispositions together make up the political military potential of states. The stronger and more diffuse the first attitude, the greater the likelihood that a state will respond to an appropriate outside stimulus by cultivating military strength and its external use. The stronger and more diffused all four attitudes are, the greater will be the tendency of the public to support any government policy aiming at the production and exertion of military power. Yet regardless of the state of these predispositions, the strength of competing demands for resources needed for other purposes is another factor which may affect the degree to which productive capacity is allotted to the military sector. The impingement of this factor depends both on the general ability of society to balance expectations and performances, which balancing is greatly facilitated by conditions of rapid economic growth, and on the acuteness with which particular non-military demands are experienced at the time. In 1967–69, for instance, the increasing demand for resources generated by the involvement of the United States in the Vietnamese war clashed sharply in the perception by a sizeable proportion of the American people of the need to solve domestic social and economic problems.

As has been noted repeatedly, however, the *actions* of government and public depend also on *situational* factors. It is therefore conceivable that public support for a *particular* military policy of the government, in a particular situation, will be weak even though political military potential is high. Conversely, public support may be extremely strong in a particular situation even though political military potential is comparatively weak. In any case, such support should be expected to be stronger on some occasions for mobilizing or using military power than on others. Political military potential only means that, when facing equal, and equally perceived and evaluated, international situations, the military response of states will vary with their degree of public support.

The conceptual scheme presented in this chapter can also accommodate the case of influential publics pressing a reluctant government to increase armaments or to resort to force internationally. This can happen when members of the government perceive and evaluate the international situation differently from an influential proportion of the public; or when menbers of the government are less "warlike" or "militarist" than the population at large; or when the government is divided or paralyzed; or when influential interest-groups urge additional armament or resort to military power.

Political Potential and Types of States

To the historian and to the contemporary observer, states differ greatly in their military political potential. Differences of this kind can reinforce or partly offset differences in economic potential or administrative competence. The question arises whether more or less political military potential tends to be associated with different types of states.

Thus, it may be asked whether political military potential tends to vary regularly with types of politcal regime. Indubitably, the influence which various parts of public can exert on the government is basically structured by the form of regime. But how the public's predispositions, which make up political military potential, are affected by the form of government is a different question; and it is not one which can be answered at the present state of research in the social sciences.

It is easy to jump to the conclusion that states with authoritarian or totalitarian regimes have a political military potential superior to that of liberal democratic states. A government in an authoritarian state may be said not to need public support; it can simply command acceptance of its allocative decisions; and a totalitarian government may be thought to command the power to mold public attitudes to its desire, as well as direct, by means of controlling relevant information, the situational responses of the public. However, leaving aside the question of whether public obedience and voluntary public support are identical in their effect on the moblization of military strength, authoritarian and totalitarian governments can be strong or weak, as can be democratic governments. Various elites, which form the most influential part of the public, may be divided on situational responses, and differ in the antecedent dispositions that make up military political potential. Nor is it necessary for a strong authoritarian government to have a strong disposition to seek military solutions of international disputes, or to be aggressive in the use of military strength for acquisitive ends. Authoritarian governments have often been weak (*e.g.,* the Ottoman empire around 1900, or the Austro-Hungarian monarchy in 1914). Numerous defections of Soviet citizens during the early phases of World War II revealed that the hold of Stalin's government on the public was then precarious. Turning to democratic regimes, during World War II, the British and American publics strongly supported the war effort against the Axis powers; but the British public was divided when the governments launched a military expedition against Egypt in 1956, and the American public became increasingly divided as the war in Vietnam dragged on in 1968.

This is not to say that differences in political regime have no impact on political military potential. But problems of comparability may not permit a statistical testing of relationshps between form of government and this base of military potential. If such a relationship exists at all, the extent of historical diversity suggests that it is weak. The fact is that the propensity to mobilize and use military force internationally is an element of political culture which, one presumes, may be strong or weak under any form of political regime.

The predisposition to support the national community depends on the extent to which the population is politically integrated which—as Belgium and Algeria, on the one hand, and Spain and Hungary, on the other hand, exemplify—can be large or small under quite different regimes. The public disposition to support the foreign and military government because it is authoritative once again can occur to a greater or lesser extent under different regimes. And so can personal or special group interest in a strong military policy. In socialist countries, to be sure, it is less likely that economic interest groups are strong supporters of such a policy. But there is no reason to assume that other special interests (e.g., professional military interests) cannot occur under all forms of government. It is also possible (and indeed plausible, although no empirical studies point this way) that the overall performance of government in meeting public expectations has a stronger bearing on support of military policy than the *form* of government.

The relationship between stage of economic development and political military potential has also remained unexplored. It is easy to find examples of high and low political potential in highly developed as well as economically underdeveloped countries. However, taking the less developed states at the present time as a group, they evidently lag behind the more developed states in the degree to which populations are politically integrated within the framework of the sovereign state. There are a few highly developed countries which are afflicted with troublesome ethnic division (e.g., Belgium and Canada), but a large proportion of the underdeveloped countries, especially among the new states, are at this time conspicuously weak in any broad-based sense of "national" solidarity. In many economically underdeveloped countries (e.g., Burma, the Congo), moreover, a large proportion of the population is so little related to the central government, let alone its foreign and military policy, that the question of the public support or opposition has correspondingly little meaning. Yet this situation is far from uniform. Some economically less developed countries have been or are governed by leaders or political parties capable of generating a high degree of the kind of political unity on which political potential for military strength rests. As the example of Nkrumah in Ghana, Nasser in the U.A.R., and Sukarno in Indonesia indicate, such unity may be temporary if it is the product of essentially personal leadership. Unity rests on a more solid foundation where a political party achieves a political monopoly and—by means of organization, indoctrination, and perhaps terror—succeeds in destroying traditional and divisive political, economic, and social structures, and in mobilizing the masses of the population for the political goals of the regime. Communist China, North Korea and North Vietnam are examples of such development.

On the other hand, one may wonder whether the predisposition to rely on military force for the purpose of solving international conflicts does not tend to diminish in the economically very advanced communities. This propensity seems to be extremely weak at this time in Britain, France, Germany, the Lowlands, the Scandinavian countries, Italy, Switzerland, Austria, Canada, Japan, and in most of the communist states of eastern Europe. Only the United States and the U.S.S.R., in this category of economically highly developed states, are using military force with frequency. But these exceptions do not necessarily argue agains such a trend since these two states, which excel in military power, occupy special positions of leadership in the structure of the international system, and since—it is plausible to assume—the tendency to give up the appeal to arms may be least powerful where the sheer magnitude of available military capabilities abets the disposition to resort to force internationally. But whether such a trend exists must at this time remain an open question. It may be asked further whether very high and rising levels of education, which are associated with an advanced state of economic and technological development, do not tend to increase public perception and evaluation of international conflict, and thus increase the weight of situational factors against that of the predispositions which make up political military potential. This need not mean that the majorities of populations assume this participatory posture regarding problems of foreign and military policy. The trend, if it exists, would be significant even if the minority, which was so inclinced before, has increased appreciably with economic and educational growth. That such a trend exists is a plausible hypothesis. Finally, there were abundant signs in the 1960's that the sheer ability of government *qua* authority to command popular support for policies was declining in the industirally advanced societies in favor of authority based on competence and performance in problem solving. This development could also be seen as rooted in increasing affluence and education, and reflecting a spreading disposition to judge governments on the pros and cons of performance in particular situations.

Even five years ago, there was a tendency to contrast the political stability of the technologically advanced societies with the instability of most economically less developed countries, and the temptation to infer that, for this reason alone, the former tended to have a political potential for military strength decisively superior to that of the latter as a class. However, neither the premise nor the inference can be sustained by observation. Political stability is perfectly compatible with a weakening of the four predispositions with which we have identified a strong political basis for military strength. In fact, it is clear that the first disposition is at this time remarkably low in most European countries, in Canada and Japan. As we have argued, there is in this class of countries also a tendency of situational responses to gain weight relative to the dispositional factors, and perhaps for governments to receive less support first because they are the constituted authorities. Furthermore, civil-right riots in the United States and student rebellion in the United States, France, West Germany,

Italy, Japan, and other advanced countries are phenomena which cast doubt on the premise as well. Events in Czechoslovakia in 1968 indicated that the older Communist countries were by no means exempt from such developments. At this time, it seems quite possible that the vaunted political stability in the highly developed countries is subject to forceful challenges. And unless these challenges are met constructively, the political cohesion of these countries may sharply decrease. To conclude, although all three constituents of military strength are subject to change in the contemporary world, the political foundation no less than economic and administrative potential, our understanding of what brings these changes about varies from one constituent to another. Roughly speaking, these differences in understanding parallel the unequal development of the social sciences: economics, the theory of public administration, and the cluster of academic disciplines concerned with political, social and cultural life. We manage to identify the conditions producing economic and technological growth reasonably well. We are less well off in comprehending those bases of administrative competence which are not a direct result of economic and technological progress. We have succeeded least in elucidating the springs of politico-cultural change, and are often surprised and baffled by its manifestations. But even these factors are less mysterious than they were not so very long ago, and the hope runs strong that the mysteries will yield increasingly to the labors of professional research.